The Sacred Dance

Spiritual Opportunities of

Marriage

The Sacred Dance

Spiritual Opportunities of

Marriage

Larry Wampler, Ph.D.

BEACH STONE PRESS
ENCINITAS, CALIFORNIA

The Sacred Dance: Spiritual Opportunities of Marriage

For information, contact

Beach Stone Press
P.O. Box 234074
Leucadia, CA 92023-4074
    www.beachstonepress.com
    www.drlarrywampler.com

Cover design by Gertrud Mueller Nelson
Text design and text and cover layout by Robert Goodman, Silvercat™,
San Diego, California

Swan images on front cover by William Morris

Library of Congress Control Number: 2007908866
isbn 978-0-9801365-1-7

printed in the United States of America

To my parents, Frieda and Thornton, for their

example of love and respect (through more than

seventy years of marriage) and to my wife,

Kathy, for her constant support and inspiration

Acknowledgments

Many people contributed helpful advice and encouragement. In addition to my wife, Kathy, I especially want to thank Conrad Herring and Gertrud Mueller Nelson, who read multiple drafts and provided invaluable editorial advice. I am also grateful to my agent, Janet Rosen (at the Sheree Bykofsky Literary Agency), for her patience and loyalty.

Contents

Preface

Everybody wants to go to heaven, but nobody wants to die. Likewise, in hope of a heavenly marriage, we all want to change our partners, but we don't want to change ourselves. This book will help you see your mate not merely as someone who either fulfills or frustrates your desires, but as someone uniquely equipped to help you change for the good. This new perspective opens a door to the soulful partnership you dreamed of when you first fell in love.

Most marital self-help books deny the inevitable tension of close relationship. They insinuate that marital problems result from plain ignorance and incompetence, needing correction from a qualified authority. Hardly anyone disputes the benefit of acquiring certain relationship skills. Yet, this pragmatic approach imposes a vision of marriage that is both inflated and impoverished.

It caters to the popular ideal of marriage as a permanent state of contentment — if only we could get it right. Unable to achieve this fanciful goal, many couples feel like failures. Still, they persist in tilting at windmills, clinging to the impossible dream of a carefree, "happy" marriage. This vain ambition obscures a more promising reality: Marriage amounts to a strenuous program of personal and spiritual transformation.

Unlike the typical marital self-help manual, this book offers no quick fixes for couples willing to settle for peaceful coexistence. You will find no ammunition to bolster a demand that your spouse behave in a certain way, on the authority of the latest expert. *The Sacred Dance* takes you deeper. It presents a vision for personal and spiritual awakening through intensive relationship. You will discover how radical intimacy infuses marriage — and sex, in particular — with lasting vitality.

As a psychotherapist working with spiritually oriented clients, I often see a connection between psychological and spiritual development. Growth in one domain bolsters growth in the other. Sometimes the two appear indistinguishable. Psychotherapy and spirituality share the ambitious goal of transforming consciousness. Both delve beneath the surface reality, to find a deeper truth. Both address the need to overcome social conditioning. Both seek the proper balance between self and other people. Both require self-discipline.

In marriage especially, psychological skills pay spiritual dividends. Do you know how to calm yourself when you get upset? Then you'll be able to forestall the escalation of many domestic quarrels. That, in turn, facilitates spiritual growth by allowing time to see your frustrations in perspective, beyond the immediate provocation from your partner. In recognition of this common ground, psychological and spiritual considerations intertwine throughout the chapters ahead.

The Sacred Dance features many practical suggestions you can put to use, with or without your partner's collaboration. Vivid examples, drawn from my personal and professional experience, show how. This does not require major upheaval in your life. Small shifts in attitude and modest adjustments in behavior can enrich your marriage and deepen your spirituality.

This book portrays a spirituality of marriage, without assuming any particular creed or religion. Still, it mainly draws on Judeo-Christian sources. That's my tradition, by birth and individual history. Surpassing any personal reasons, everyone growing up in America feels the weight of our predominant religious heritage. Whether we examine it or ignore it, accept it or reject it, this cultural legacy inescapably colors our attitudes about love, marriage and sexuality. Bible quotations are offered *not* on authority, as revealed truth, but rather on their merits, as testable propositions, subject to confirmation in your experience.

Furthermore, Christianity has special relevance to the spirituality of marriage because of its unparalleled emphasis on love. All the essential Christian principles revolve around love: (1) God loves us, without exception; (2) We honor God by simply receiving this unconditional love, or *grace*; and (3) God calls us to love generously, in response. Setting aside other potentially divisive Christian doctrines, who would stand against love? Love measures any spiritual aspiration.

Many people of good will cannot easily assent to the idea of a personal God. If you prefer, substitute some other abstraction, such as a Higher Power. The implications for a spirituality of marriage remain unchanged. What we *do* matters more than what we *believe*.

Introduction

Marriage and the
Spirituality of Everyday Life

Our culture tends to confine spirituality to solemn matters of religious belief and practice, distinct from our daily routines of work and play. According to this notion, attending religious services, reading scripture and praying qualify as "spiritual," but walking the dog, making love and performing household chores do not.

Spirituality beckons, as well, in the ordinary activities of married life. Consider, for example, Greg and Cindy as they set out to repaint their bathroom. First they have to choose from a staggering array of colors, including thirty-seven different tints of "white."

Greg hurriedly makes his choice, as Cindy settles down on a stool in front of the color charts at the paint store. "This 'eggshell' ought to do the trick," he suggests.

Cindy furrows her brow. "Hmmm. This one called Navajo looks pretty good to me, too."

"OK. Sure. I'll go with that."

"No, wait. I didn't mean to necessarily *choose* that one," Cindy protests. "I'm still looking."

"Whatever. Let's just pick one and get going. We have a lot of work ahead."

"Not so fast. We'll have to live with this color for a long time. I want to consider all the options."

"Tell me you're kidding." Greg's heel taps impatiently. "White is white. They all look fine to me."

"Can't you see the difference? Eggshell has a warm, golden tint. The Navajo looks more pinkish."

"Yeah, fine. So which do you want?"

"Well, I'm not sure. Among the whites, I prefer the cooler tints. But now I'm beginning to consider these pale blues in the next section."

"You're driving me nuts," Greg exclaims a little too loudly. "You choose a color. I'm going over to get the brushes... unless you need to be there to check the bristles."

"Oh, Greg, don't be that way."

Finally arriving home with their supplies, Greg and Cindy discover they have very different ideas about how to proceed with the job. Now, Cindy is the one more eager to forge ahead. She wants to start right in applying paint, while Greg insists on filling all the tiny cracks, then sanding and cleaning the walls. He thinks they should also mask the glass and tile, which Cindy judges a ridiculous waste of time. They're just getting started, and already they both feel unappreciated and disrespected.

Like most couples, Greg and Cindy hate to fight. Right now especially, they need each other's cooperation to accomplish the task at hand. So why are they bickering about small matters?

Couples quarrel over seemingly trivial concerns in defense of personal principles they hold dear. Not lofty principles, perhaps, but worthy principles with surprising spiritual significance. Like Greg and Cindy, everybody yearns to feel appreciated for a good idea or a job well done. Everybody wants to do things her own way, sometimes.

On the surface, these concerns look petty. We rarely admit to caring about them. Still, over the long term in a committed relationship, they become legitimate matters of integrity. They represent dawning virtues: standing up for truth and justice, exercising personal power in the face of opposition. Most arguments over who's "right" really hinge on competing claims for respect — between two people poorly equipped to confer it on themselves.

The inevitable conflicts of marriage prod each of us to forge a distinct identity, and consolidate our integrity. We need this sturdy, *separate* self in order to tolerate intense intimacy, permitting romance to ripen into love. By illuminating our weaknesses and insecurities, every conflict or disappointment in marriage actually represents a spiritual opportunity. We ordinarily shrink from opportunities like these, but spiritual awakening requires willingness to accept the transformative power of ordeal.

We're drawn to marriage in pursuit of inner wholeness, and unity with something beyond ourselves. We persist through hard times because of our inborn desire to give and receive love. As Bruce Springsteen put it, "Everybody's got a hungry heart." These are clearly spiritual aspirations.

Spirituality expresses the deepest meaning of life. It invites us to embrace the full truth about ourselves and the world we live in. It calls for ethical conduct and lifelong personal development. It prompts a search for meaning in suffering and death. Above all, spirituality aims to fulfill our transcendent existence in relation to something greater than ourselves.

From this perspective, we see the world afresh. We realize our kinship with the rest of creation. All the traditional virtues spring from this foundation: humility, thankfulness, generosity, forgiveness, peace, hope and especially love. Here, we can rise above past regrets and future anxieties to live in the present, where God resides.

Spiritual practice encompasses any activity that brings out our best, true selves, while reminding us of our essential links to other people and to God. When we recognize transcendent meaning in ordinary events, this is spirituality. When we respond to that meaning by way of our routine conduct, this is spirituality. Marriage presents unique opportunities for this type of spiritual realization.

Part One of *The Sacred Dance* introduces the Spirituality of Marriage, showing how it qualifies as a "vocation" in the Western religious tradition. A survey of the mysteries of love reveals their unique power to open our hearts and mobilize spiritual awakening. Married life presents potent exercises that cultivate universal spiritual virtues, such as thankfulness, humility, forgiveness and compassion.

In Part Two, you'll discover the Five Qualifications needed to capitalize on these spiritual opportunities: self-commitment, wholesome shame, desire to live a shared life, tolerance for conflict, and appreciation for mystery and paradox. These qualifications are not severe. They mostly rely on sheer willingness. Are you willing to transcend yourself by plunging more deeply into relationship? Then read on.

Part One

The Spirituality of Marriage

Love is ... the fundamental and innate vocation of every human being.
—John Paul II[1]

Every expression of love amounts to a spiritual event. Even our most flawed, human attempts echo their Source and link us to God. For thousands of years, Western religions have recognized marriage as the prime symbol for the covenant of love between God and humankind.

This is usually taken to mean that married couples should try to imitate God's faithful love and God's willingness to forgive. But couples who know where to look will find an even deeper correspondence between married love and spirituality. They take up a Sacred Dance that transcends individual existence, and carries them both to God.

These couples make a commitment to personal and spiritual transformation, through the joys and rigors of shared life. They strive for deep intimacy, mutual surrender, and a fruitful expression of unified will. They pledge to persevere through any hardship.

This perspective casts new light on the routine conflicts of married life. While always seeking harmony, partners in the Sacred Dance accept the likelihood of some disappointment and frustration. These trials are the natural agencies of self-discovery, emotional healing, intimate encounter — and spiritual development.

Marriage presents unique spiritual opportunities because our mates and God reach out to us in similar ways. The four chapters in Part One show how both God and our mates solicit love, intimacy, surrender, integrity and more. First, we'll probe the mysteries of love, revealing their curious power to transform our hearts. Then you'll see how marriage offers ideal conditions for spiritual vocation: a disciplined way of life that builds virtue and invites spiritual awakening.

One

The Mysteries of Love

A single vivid experience of love will advance us much farther, will far more surely protect our souls from evil, than the most arduous struggle against sin. — Alexander Yelchaninov[1]

Whenever we practice love, we draw near to God. We transcend ourselves, casting our lot with all the men and women throughout history who have served as channels of God's grace in the world. We also transcend time. Everything else that we do or make or say or become will eventually perish. But every act of love endures forever, because it resonates with the eternal and infinite God.

Still, who can fathom love? It routinely defies our expectations. No simple definition can contain it. In English, we have only one word for love. It stretches thin to cover the full range from a mother's unwavering concern, to a giddy, teenage infatuation. Love between a husband and wife is perhaps the most complex of all. It embraces everything from passionate desire to quiet companionship, from self-sacrifice to an acceptance of permission to "use" each other.

Other languages are better endowed to speak of love. Greek assigns different words to distinguish four varieties of love: One term refers to the warm, affectionate love between old friends or kin. Another designates lustful desire. A third type of love expresses devotion to another person's welfare, even at the sacrifice of self-interest. And finally, erotic love seeks union, in the pursuit of self-fulfillment. These are useful distinctions, but none of them can fully capture a true life experience. Married love, at its best, includes all four types—and more.

Symbols such as wedding rings, Valentine hearts, paintings and other works of art open another window onto love. But if these symbols seem to provide a clearer impression, it's because they avoid specifying all the complexity they imply. They depend on the beholder's imagination to fill in the gaps. We glimpse love but we cannot pin it down.

As soon as we think we have identified some quintessential feature of love, its opposite arises to confound us. We may imagine love in terms of joy and peace, but it just as easily stirs up turmoil. Love calls forth the beast along with the saint in each of us. Love invites us to receive, as much as it inspires giving. Love sometimes relies on an act of will; at other times, it overtakes us, arriving as a free gift. Love overlooks faults; then it magnifies them. In order to harness the spiritual power of love, we must give up some pious and sentimental notions to make room for these sobering ironies.

Love Draws Out the Best and the Worst in Us

Love is a favorite literary theme. Many classic novels and biographies tell of courage and devotion inspired by love. In the best of these accounts, heroic love intertwines with quirks of character and circumstance, so that we cannot tell precisely where love lapses into something less noble.

These impurities range from simple human frailty to sordid displays of jealousy, manipulation, betrayal, deceit, obsession and violence. The dark side of love often predominates in the great romantic stories of literature, such as Romeo and Juliet, Antony and Cleopatra, David and Bathsheba, Psyche and Eros. This is partly because tragic flaws make good drama. Even more, it reflects the inescapable shortcomings of human nature inflamed by love. True-to-life examples expose the absurdity in sentimental ideals of perfect love.

After two years of marriage, Joel and Yvonne still can't get enough of each other. Their old friends finally gave up inviting either one separately. If Joel and Yvonne can't go out together, they don't care to go at all. They even shop for groceries together.

On weekdays, they talk by phone several times, and meet for lunch whenever possible. Occasionally, one drops in at the other's workplace. Their troubles begin on one of these surprise visits.

Everyone in Yvonne's office knows Joel, so he breezes past the busy receptionist with a wave and a smile, and sets out in search of his wife. On his way down the hall to her office, he catches a fleeting glimpse of someone dressed like Yvonne, through the tall, narrow window in the meeting room door.

By the time the image registers, Joel's momentum has carried him a couple steps past the door. He stops short, confused: "That *looked* like Yvonne, from behind — same blue skirt and white blouse she's wearing today, same general outline — but it can't be her. Some man had his arm around that woman, and his face buried in her neck."

Joel hears a sudden commotion in the meeting room, followed by a thump and a loud crack. He turns back and throws the door open, to reveal Yvonne on the floor, half under the conference table, with a strange man sprawled on top of her. A chair is overturned. Papers lie scattered on the floor.

"What's going on here?" Joel demands.

Yvonne and the stranger look up at Joel, then back at each other — and burst out laughing. "Are you OK?" they ask simultaneously. After more laughter and mutual assurances, they scramble awkwardly to their feet, looking disheveled and embarrassed.

Joel doesn't like the look of it, and he doesn't like being ignored. "I said, 'What's going on here?'"

"Don't worry. I'm all right." Yvonne bends down to pick up some papers.

"Yeah, well who's this guy?"

Only now, she realizes Joel has concerns beyond her risk of injury. She casts a disapproving look. "Calm down, and I'll introduce you."

The stranger steps forward, his right hand extended. "I'm Bill Newman, from the consulting firm of Riley & Newman. And you are...?"

"...the husband," Joel says, disregarding the proffered handshake.

Yvonne intervenes to break the tension. "Maybe we could finish our work tomorrow, Bill."

"Uh, sure." He hurriedly gathers his coat and briefcase and backs out the door, saying, "I'm sorry for any misunderstanding."

"Don't give it a thought. See you tomorrow," Yvonne calls out in the direction of his retreat. Then, turning to Joel, her tone chills: "What's the matter with you? I've never seen you act so rude. You embarrassed me in front of a business associate."

"Well, you have to admit it looked pretty bad — you sprawled on the floor, and charming Billy all over you."

"Are you insane? I don't know what you *think* you saw, but until just a moment before you burst in, Bill and I were leaning over the table, looking at the reorganization proposal we commissioned from his firm. Then he reached behind me for some other papers, lost his balance, and we both toppled over. Anything beyond that is purely your imagination."

Joel compares this account to his mental snapshot of Bill and Yvonne, finding a likely correspondence at the point where Bill reached behind her. "Oh," he says sheepishly. "I guess I misread what was going on. But I still don't trust that guy alone with you."

"The point is whether you trust *me* alone with him. Even if Bill — or anybody else — were to make a pass at me, do you really think I'd be receptive?"

"Probably not. You've never given me reason to be suspicious. But you've never been betrayed like I have, either. I don't know what came over me. I love you so much, it makes me crazy sometimes."

"It was crazy, all right. But it doesn't feel like love to me."

Yvonne is right. Her husband's jealousy arises not from love, but insecurity. Love only sets the stage. Joel leaped to the wrong conclusion because he secretly fears that he is unworthy of Yvonne. He can easily imagine her choosing someone else, given the opportunity. His desire for constant togetherness partly reflects his dread of competition. With Joel's possessiveness laid bare, Yvonne feels less flattered by his desire to keep her continually in sight. She will likely chafe under the constraint, seeking time apart to fend off the implied slur against her fidelity.

This incident shows how love illuminates our failings and past hurts, along with our virtues and strengths. Love incites conflict, spurring change. We need not feel ashamed that our best efforts result in such imperfect love. How else could we grow, except by putting our hearts on the line, submitting to the humbling ordeal that love thrusts upon us? For the sake of love, we work to overcome our weaknesses. In this way, love prompts us toward our highest fulfillment.

Love Inspires Giving and Receiving

Giving is a traditional hallmark of love. We offer whatever we have for the sake of our beloved, whose needs become priorities of our own. We actively promote each other's welfare, even at considerable self-sacrifice. Only love can inspire such generosity.

In addition to giving (attention, support, acceptance, etc.), we must learn how to receive, and even how to *take*. Love entitles us to assert bold claims. Unless you insist that your partner take your concerns seriously, love cannot flourish.

Over a period of several months, Joanne repeatedly complains to her husband that she feels overwhelmed by all the duties of parenting, housework and her stressful job. Bob usually responds sympathetically with a few words of encouragement, or a warm hug. Occasionally, he volunteers a helping hand.

"I'm just so exhausted, I could cry," Joanne laments one night after dinner.

"You *do* look tired. Why don't you go lie down, while I wash the dishes?"

"Thanks. I will."

Joanne drags herself to the living room, and collapses on the sofa. There, upon reflection, her grateful attitude breaks down. "Wait a minute. His offer isn't really so generous. I planned the meal, I shopped for the groceries, and I cooked the dinner, as usual. It's only fair that he should clean up."

Joanne feels a twinge of guilt as she starts down this resentful line of thinking. She doesn't want to grumble. She's tired, irritable and confused. But she has no chance to sort her feelings, because at that moment, three-year-old Billy climbs on top of her, planting his sharp little knee right below her ribs.

"Unhh," Joanne groans. "Not so hard on Mommy's tummy, Sweetheart."

Meanwhile, five-year-old Megan is tugging at her arm. "Come play a game with us, Mommy."

Joanne smiles weakly. "OK, but just one. Then, you both need baths."

The next night, Joanne feels no less weary. So after dinner, she tries again to solicit Bob's help in devising a solution.

"I feel bad that I complain so much about being tired," she begins.

"That's all right. I understand."

"No, it's *not* all right. And I think you *don't* understand," Joanne insists, gathering steam. "I'm trying to tell you that I can't go on like this. I feel like I don't have a minute to myself. Every morning when the alarm goes off, I'm still so exhausted I can barely face the day."

"Well, as a matter of fact, I was hoping we could get to bed early tonight. You probably need a little of the same thing I do." Bob arches one eyebrow, making his best devilish grin.

Joanne sighs in exasperation. "I'm sure you're right. I'd like to make love more often, if I had any energy left for it. Something has to give."

"I'll bet you've had another hard day at work," Bob says in a consoling tone. "So thank God it's Friday. Tomorrow will be better."

"You're just patronizing me," Joanne shoots back. "Your words sound great, but nothing ever changes."

This remark offends Bob, but he restrains himself from making a hostile comeback. He hopes this won't turn into a fight, spoiling their prospects for sex. "Well, what do you want *me* to do?" he asks, with an edge of irritation in his voice. "I work hard, too, you know."

Joanne sighs again. "Of course you do. Sometimes I think I'm just inadequate." She falls silent for a few moments fending off this false judgment against herself, before it can undermine her resolve. "Still, you could help out a lot more. Maybe you could put the kids to bed once in a while."

"But they always want you," Bob counters.

"That's true, but maybe they'd quit clinging to me if you took care of them more. All I know for sure is that I'm getting crushed under the workload, and I need more of your help."

"Well, as a start in that direction, why don't I put Megan and Bobby to bed right now, while you go draw a bath for us? But don't get in it, because you know they won't settle down unless I promise you'll come up to tuck them in."

"Fair enough . . . for now. Tomorrow, when we're both fresh, I want to talk about a long-term solution."

How do you imagine Bob and Joanne will settle this matter? He could agree to do more of the parenting and household chores on a regular basis rather than waiting for a desperate plea from his wife. Or they could decide to get along with less money, enabling Joanne to work only part-time, as she would prefer. Maybe nothing will change until Joanne unilaterally cuts back on housework, provoking a crisis that captures Bob's attention. In any event, she makes the essential first step — for herself and for the sake of their marriage —in demanding that Bob take her complaints seriously, and participate in finding a joint solution.

If one partner has a problem, then the couple has a problem. Like Joanne, you must insist that your partner find *some* way, according to his own style, of responding to your needs. Some people misconstrue this as selfishness. To the contrary, it is both a right and a duty of marriage, exercised for mutual benefit.

Receiving love is often more difficult than giving. First, we must expose our raw need, doing whatever it takes to gain notice. Then we have to endure the dependent position of accepting indulgence.

Does Love Overtake Us, or Is Love Hard Work?

Two rival versions of love compete for our allegiance. One appeals to our hearts; the other appeals to our heads. Popular movies portray a love that sweeps us off our feet, and carries us to delirious heights of passion. Critics of this view insist that real love requires a rational decision, followed by a lot of hard work.

Most authorities side with the latter point of view, stressing the effort and self-discipline required to love well. Yet, this idea of love is very chilly. It leaves out the ingredients that make love so compelling: hypnotic focus, intoxicating passion, and spontaneous self-transcendence. These involuntary experiences are among the mainstays of spiritual power. We cannot dismiss them as mere trifles of romantic delusion. They will not be denied.

Love always arrives unexpectedly, even when we have earnestly courted it. No one can extort love. Anyone who claims to have *earned* love exposes a failure to comprehend it. We cannot predict the exact form love will assume, or how it will unfold over the course of a married lifetime. When love alights, we wonder, "Why me? Why am I so blessed?"

"When you two first fell in love, what attracted you to each other?" I ask this question of every couple who consults me for counseling. Few have a ready reply. This is only partly owing to the difficulty of recalling the original source of attraction from within a current state of alienation. Even for people who can muster an answer, the reasons are usually vague:

She seemed to understand me like nobody else.
I felt safe with him, as if we had known each other for years.
It was mostly physical—her good looks overwhelmed me.
I just remember gazing into his eyes, spellbound.

These responses raise more questions than they answer. What accounts for the easy rapport or the immediate sense of security? Why *this* beautiful woman and not another? What made *this* man's eyes so hypnotic? No one can say for sure.

Love discriminates. It pulls us in unexpected directions, sometimes against our will, and contrary to rational judgment. Someone who has suffered a broken heart may resolve to choose more sensibly next time, only to fall for a vagabond. One suitor inspires delight, while another —equally attractive by any objective standard —fails to kindle a spark. The heart has a mind of its own. This does not relieve us of responsibility for our actions. But yet, we cannot fully manage our affections. Love offers itself as a gift, like a seed that unaccountably sprouts in its appointed season.

Of course, love also requires careful tending in order to bear good fruit. How can we provide for the needs of our beloved, except by devoting some effort? How can we remain appealing and stimulating except by taking care of ourselves? Without continuing nurture, love withers as surely as a plant deprived of water.

But gentle nurture easily lapses into a campaign to compel change. The enterprising American spirit teaches us to mistrust current reality. We tend to equate acceptance of the status quo with complacent tolerance for defects. So we try to seize control. We cannot succeed in storming the gates of heaven, though. Anyone who sets out with steely determination to *improve* his marriage, or (worse) to reform his partner, will strangle the process and warp the outcome.

We might better foster love's development by cherishing everything good and beautiful in what already exists, the same as if to foster the growth of a child. Or to use a spiritual metaphor, we can open our hearts to conversion. While we have an active part to play, we cannot control love. Some of the most important forces operate beyond our reach or comprehension. The mystery of love will have its way with us, without regard for logic, justice or intent.

Love Is Blind, but Mariage Restores Its Sight

Over the course of childhood, every person unconsciously assembles a complex self-image, based partly on the countless directives received from parents and other authorities defining what's acceptable and what's not. This self-image is more or less narrow and rigid, depending on the severity of our upbringing. For example, when parents demand too much hard work from their children, at the expense of play, the forbidden impulses are pushed into unconsciousness. All kinds of scorned childhood features and unmet childhood needs likewise retreat into darkness.

Gender plays an important role in this process, as every society elaborates distinct models of what's appropriate for males and females. In America, we still consider gentleness more appealing in women than in men. We admire a measure of aggressiveness in men, but judge it unseemly in women.

Alienated from vital parts of ourselves, we ache for completion, and feel driven to find our "other half." Sexual attraction always contains an element of desire for reunion with these disavowed qualities of our own. We unwittingly project them onto someone else who offers suitable hooks to hang them on. This process has been termed *projective identification*, because we identify with the parts of ourselves we project onto another person, who then exerts magnetic allure.

To the extent a man defines himself in macho terms such as intimidating strength, he feels attracted to stereotypically "feminine" women who appear delicate, sensitive and vulnerable — so much the better if they're endowed with large breasts, as palpable badges of femininity. To the extent a woman fails to realize her own power, she likely makes a complementary projection. Thus, the attraction is mutual.

The more of ourselves we have repudiated, the more intensely attracted we feel to someone who embodies our disowned characteristics. This partly explains why opposites attract. A quiet, cautious man pairs up with a flashy, spirited woman. Her spontaneity enchants him, while she feels drawn to his apparent depth and self-control.

Actually, both struggle with self-doubt. They merely employ different strategies to cope with it. She covers her insecurity with glib words and deeds. He strives to mentally resolve all uncertainty before risking any action. Each mistakenly attributes self-assurance to the other. Feeling insufficient, they unconsciously try to complete themselves by way of sexual alliance with someone who seems to carry what they lack.

In the same way, someone timidly passive finds mutual attraction with a decisive, controlling person. Someone rigid and scrupulous pairs up with another who is cavalier about rules. *Love* makes the strangest bedfellows.

These projections cannot withstand the test of prolonged contact over years spent living together. "Love is blind, but marriage restores its sight."[2] Gradually, both parties discover to their dismay that they are living with a complex, multidimensional, confoundedly imperfect person, rather than the pleasing caricature they had imagined. In the harsh light of intimate daily encounter, formerly appealing features are perceived as irritating defects. Her emotional displays — once so refreshing — begin to look self-indulgent and flighty. His previously admirable discipline now appears stuffy and boring.

These realizations come as rude disappointments. People feel betrayed. Typically, they set about trying to reform their partners to become more like themselves. The effort usually proves futile, provoking frustration on one side, and hurt feelings on the other. In the unlikely event of "successfully" coercing change, they will have extinguished all passionate chemistry.

Yet, disenchantment brings two spiritual opportunities: First, rather than trying to remake our partners, we can take up the challenge to love an actual, whole person. This ultimately proves much more satisfying than chasing a mirage. Even more, by cultivating an attitude of wonder and appreciation for what seems alien in our partners, we open the way to reclaim lost aspects of ourselves. See-ing through our romantic delusions, we realize they have not misled us so badly. Who would voluntarily embark on such a daunting spiritual quest, were it not for the allure of infatuation?

Like God, love works in mysterious ways. Here, you have seen how love brings out the best *and* the worst in people; how it calls for gracious receiving as much as generous giving; how it sometimes requires disciplined effort, while at other times goading us to re-linquish control; how it uncovers sacred truths by way of beguiling illusions. Through our participation in these mysteries, we invoke the redemptive power of love.

Two

The Redemptive Power of Love

Beloved, let us love one another; for love is of God, and he who loves is born of God and knows God. He who does not love does not know God; for God is love. — 1st John 4:7–8[1]

Our entire Western religious tradition rests on two brief guidelines: Love God; and Love your neighbor as yourself.[2] How can *married* love help us fulfill these spiritual mandates? How might even erotic love foster spiritual growth?

Loving God

The lofty ambition to love God finds remarkable parallels in marriage. (1) Like God, our mates reach out for trust under high-risk conditions. (2) Like God, our mates invite surrender to faithful, committed love. (3) Like God, our mates stretch our imaginations to apprehend their gradually unfolding complexity. (4) Like God, our mates inspire self-improvement. The same motif echoes throughout this book: *In marriage, we discover how to love God.*

21

Love nurtures trust in pursuit of intimacy

Throughout history, people with a mystical bent have searched for ways to draw near to God. Not content to merely learn *about* God, or avoid offending God, they burned to *know* God in personal relationship.[3] They tried to engage God in conversation, or prayer. They practiced contemplation to quiet mind and body, the better to hear "the still, small voice" of God. They studied scripture. They lead a simple lifestyle to avoid worldly distraction.

Marriage opens a complementary new approach. In marriage, we have a chance to cultivate the attitudes, insights and capabilities needed to glimpse God. We learn now to meet God by practicing intimate relationship with another person. This provides experience taking risks, in order to build trust. All intimacy hinges on the willingness to take a risk—like revealing your true self, or asking for more than you deserve. So your relationship with God is likely no closer than your best relationship with another person.

Most people try to limit how much they have to trust either God or a human partner. In daring to disclose our true selves, or express our needs, we face our vulnerability. "Will my secrets be used against me? Can I count on support when I need it most?" We fear to trust even our own judgment. "What if I'm making a terrible mistake? How can I know whether this amounts to courage or foolishness?" In fact, we can't be certain.

Over the course of long-term, intimate encounter with a mate, we discover what it means to trust. We usually accomplish this incrementally, taking successively deeper risks, and carefully gauging the response. Do your disclosures meet with respect, or shaming and exploitation? Does your partner reciprocate with revelations of his own, or remain aloof? Can you rely on confidentiality? Can your partner keep a promise? When disappointed with your partner, can you *trust yourself* to do what's needed?

Weighing these outcomes, we set an agreeable pace of steadily deepening intimacy. Disregarding them, unfounded expectations breed disappointment and broken faith. To the extent we find the courage to take risks and build trust in marriage, we gain experience that facilitates our approach to God.

You might think that God already knows every detail that has shaped each individual existence. But intimacy develops out of voluntary disclosure and shared experience, in an atmosphere of respect for privacy. To earn our trust, God relies on our self-presentation, and openness to receive without preconception.

This is not to say that God is coy or passive. God patiently pursues us, making subtle advances. At times, we might fairly characterize God as seductive, partially revealing some enticing grace, then withdrawing to await our response.

While trust ordinarily develops little by little, it sometimes expands suddenly and dramatically, in crisis. This may happen when a couple confronts a serious illness, placing heavy demands on the more able partner. An outpouring of support in a time of desperate need gives persuasive evidence of devotion. The impact ripples throughout the relationship, inspiring deeper reliance and intimacy on every front.

Likewise, God occasionally descends like a fireball on some terrified soul who had done nothing to invite a dramatic epiphany. People singled out for divine attention can expect to be recruited for special assignment.[4] They usually meet with a demand to transcend presumed limitations, at the risk of being consumed in the process. Those who take up the challenge are forever changed by this brush with God. Trust renders them fearless. Although nothing can truly prepare us for such an extraordinary encounter, the experience of trusting your mate in a crisis affords a glimpse.

Love invites surrender

How can we express our love for God? What could God possibly want from us? Nothing less than complete access to our hearts, total dedication of our lives, and full acceptance of the blessings in store for us. This standard of total surrender might sound severe. What kind of God would give each of us individual life, and insistent powers of will, only to ask that we give it all back? How could any reasonable person venture such a comprehensive risk?

And yet, by giving ourselves only in measured portions, the deepest joy eludes us. We find freedom and fulfillment when we devote *all* that we have to some higher purpose, holding nothing in reserve. "If you would save your life, you will lose it; but if you would lose your life for my sake, you will find it."[5] This law of the universe is not reserved for prospective martyrs. It applies to all of us, every day, especially in marriage.

Just like God, our mates call us to total surrender. They want to lead us somewhere beyond our current comprehension. They want special, privileged access to our hearts. They claim our pledge of lifelong fidelity. What kind of person has the gall to insist that we "forsake all others"? At one extreme, the selfish and insecure. At the other, people in possession of self-respect, conscious of their own worth and determined to invest their lives wisely.

At the beginning of marriage, hardly anyone can sustain an attitude of surrender for very long. We start with high hopes and sincere intentions. Perhaps for the duration of a peak sexual experience, or a few minutes of intimate rapport, we present ourselves fully and completely, willing to confront any challenge, at any cost, for the sake of our beloved. But before long, we get nervous. We retreat behind our accustomed barricades, safely in control again. Like skydiving, surrender to love requires the ability to resist panic in the face of danger, staying alert and composed, even as we plunge into the unknown.

Why does surrender feel so threatening? On one hand, the prospect of surrender —whether to God or a marriage partner — threatens to expose our limitations, by putting us to the test. "What if I can't deliver what's required of me? Do I possess the necessary strength and courage? Am I worthy? Or will I suffer humiliation and rejection when my weaknesses are uncovered?"

On the other hand, the prospect of surrender — to God or to a mate — assails our pride, and threatens our independence. "I don't need anyone else telling me how to live my life. And I don't need anyone else to prop me up as I face adversity. I do just fine, making my own decisions and controlling my own destiny." Reluctant to limit our options, and fearing the loss of autonomy, we weigh the satisfactions of self-reliance against the pangs of isolation.

These are legitimate concerns. No one can offer convincing assurance to warrant a leap of faith into either spiritual or marital commitment. God generally accords us wide latitude — a lifetime of uncertain duration — in which to deliberate. Many of us try to hedge our bets as long as possible. Marriage provides a context for working our way through these momentous issues. As we adjust to love's terms within marriage, we build the strength and security needed for deeper union with God.

When Jeff and Kelly married, the nine year difference in their ages seemed trivial. He was a young thirty-five — fit and active, with a playful spirit. She was very mature for a twenty-six-year-old — earnest, ambitious and keenly focussed on her accounting career, where she was already a junior executive.

Jeff's sole concern about the age gap had hinged on the prospect of children: He already had a teenage son and daughter from a brief, early marriage. They lived with their mother, except in the summers, but he was deeply involved in their lives. "My parental instincts are completely fulfilled," he explained to Kelly. "I don't see myself raising another brood — the sleepless nights, the loss of privacy, the soccer practices. But I can imagine you might want children of your own."

Kelly had assured him of her prior, firm decision to forego motherhood. "I don't think I'm cut out for it. I'm just not the nurturing type. When you and I first got involved, I even worried about how I'd do with *your* kids. As it turns out, they're great, and I love having them in our lives. I get to be more of a big sister than a step-mom. But I cringe at the idea of little rug rats clinging to me all day. Besides, if I were to take even a couple years off from my career, I'd have to start over from the bottom. So don't worry. I'll never pressure you to have kids." Her dismissive laugh sounded so convincing.

Now, a mere five years later, at age thirty-one, everything looks different to Kelly. She has soared in her career, rising to the position of Chief Financial Officer of a small company before a change in the business climate forced it to close. Suddenly, at this natural transition point, she has become overwhelmed with longing to have a baby. She feels confused about her abrupt change of mind, and guilty about imposing it on Jeff. "Maybe it's my biological clock. Beyond that, I can't explain it. But I've never wanted anything so much."

Jeff feels bewildered, almost betrayed. "But what about your career? You always said that women who take time off for children are branded as 'soft' and lacking in job commitment."

"I'm not sure that's true anymore. Lots of women do it at some point, and these are ideal circumstances. It's not like I'm abandoning my company. So it probably wouldn't be held against me — especially in a company run by a woman CEO. Or maybe I could start my own company . . . if I go back to work at all."

Jeff's jaw drops. "What are you talking about? Where's the aspiring executive I married? The one determined to smash the glass ceiling?"

"I might still want that, but it's not everything. Certainly not the most important thing."

"Well, OK. Take some time off, if you want. With my income, and the golden parachute from your last job, we don't need the money. You can do whatever you want. Now that Justin and Stephanie are both in college, we're free. We can travel, like we've dreamed of doing. But a kid would tie us down for another twenty years."

"We can travel later. I need to get pregnant now."

"Think about it, Kelly. I'd be nearly *sixty* when the kid starts college. This is not what I signed on for. It's not what *we agreed* to do."

Tears are streaming down their faces now, as they agonize over this wrench in their well-laid plans. "I know, Jeff. It's not fair to ask this of you. But I can't let it go."

"You mean it's so important you'd let *me* go?"

"Noooooo," Kelly wails. "I don't just want a child. I want *our* child, to raise *with you*. Maybe it will be different this time, with me as your partner."

This appears to be a win-lose conflict, with little room for compromise. For Kelly to get what she so desperately wants, Jeff has to give up what he wants, and vice-versa. It would be disastrous for either of them to grudgingly concede such a vital matter; the resentment would eat them up. Perhaps they could negotiate some conditions, such as a time limit on how long they would try to conceive, but even this would put them at cross purposes. The only win-win prospect is for one party to *surrender*, fully embracing the choice, uniting with his partner's will, and resolving to making it a joint success, no looking back.

Marriage presents myriad opportunities to practice surrender. The same principles apply, on a smaller scale, when going out to dinner: you want Italian and she wants Chinese food. Or choosing where to live. Or deciding whether to open presents on Christmas Eve or in the morning.

Opportunities for surrender arise most famously in the sexual arena. Can you surrender to your partner's passion, letting yourself be transported to towering heights? Orgasm provokes a dramatic collapse of boundaries, but the event is so fleeting, we hardly have time to feel the associated threat of engulfment.

(This undoubtedly contributes to the popularity of sex, as well as the common inclination to restore some distance afterwards.) For couples who can tolerate the intensity, an even deeper inter-penetration of consciousness occurs during prolonged, eyes-open intercourse, sustaining high levels of mutual arousal, teetering on the brink of release.

Personal boundaries also blur during many other occasions of profound intimacy. In marriage, our fates are so intertwined that sorrow becomes shared sorrow, celebration becomes mutual celebration, and creation (notably in parenting) becomes joint creation. We discover how to maintain our own sense of self, even while immersed in close partnership.

All these experiences teach us that surrender leads not to an-nihilation, but expansion. Marriage serves as model and training ground for greater surrender to God, and for the more thorough-going surrender required on the occasion of death. Nothing short of death can *conquer* the ego. This side of the grave, it finds peace only in voluntary submission, resigning the quest for ascendency, in preference for union.

Love stretches the imagination

Different people respond to different aspects of God, whose infinite nature contains something to make every heart sing. Some people stand in awe of God's majestic power. Others are transfixed by the sublime mysteries of the universe. Many hardened hearts are broken open by God's compassion.

Of course, such discriminating love risks idolatry, reducing God's grandeur to smaller, more comprehensible, dimensions. In celebrat-ing God the Creator, do we deny God the Destroyer? We cannot contain God with conceptual ideas. At best, we gain a series of partial impressions through direct experience. We glimpse God's glory, and tremble. Maturing spirituality progressively expands its conception of God to embrace the terrible along with the endearing features.

In marriage, we encounter a similar problem on a human scale. We gradually uncover a staggering complexity in each other, unimaginable on our wedding day. Marriage continually challenges us to expand the borders of our love, to incorporate features in our mates that seem darkly confounding, or even repulsive. Thus, we gain experience in coming to terms with an unpredictable, uncontrollable force, with vast significance in our lives.

Love inspires self-improvement

When you open your heart to God, a process of self-examination begins. Just when you're about to do something petty or unkind, a small, inner voice arises, asking "Is this who you want to be?" Or another time, when you're feeling weak and afraid, on the brink of choosing the smaller portion in life, it inquires, "Won't you dare to claim a little more of who you are?"

Having made a commitment to serve a cause greater than ourselves, we adopt higher standards. We pay more attention to the consequences of our actions. We claim responsibility to fulfill more of our potential. Sometimes, we still fall short of our standards and our potential — perhaps more than ever, because we're risking more. But as a result of paying attention and owning responsibility, we're primed to grow.

Something very similar happens in marriage. Making such a comprehensive commitment, we become more aware of our power to choose, for better or worse. We find new motives for good conduct. Partly, of course, we want to please. Someone is watching — someone whose esteem we value. More importantly, *being loved* gives us confidence that we have something worthy to offer. When someone shows faith in us, we want to live up to it.

Above all, we realize that marriage raises the stakes. Actions take on greater significance when the yoked fate of *two* people hangs in the balance. You and your partner rely on each other to find the right steps to carry the Sacred Dance forward. If either stumbles, you both go down.

For a good example of love's power to draw out the best in a person, see the Oscar-winning movie *As Good As It Gets*. Melvin, a cranky writer, driven by obsessive-compulsive disorder, falls in love with a waitress named Carol. She treats him with kind respect despite his outrageous behavior. One day, after he has carelessly insulted her, Carol demands a compliment, as compensation. Finally, after a long pause, Melvin tells her he has started taking his medication again.

"What kind of compliment is that?" she demands to know. Melvin explains how he hates taking pills, even though his doctor had told him they could relieve many of his symptoms, and help him get along better with people. "But last week, because of you, I started taking the pills. You make me want to be a better man," he says, with conviction. Carol has to admit that's the best compliment she's ever received.

The Closest Neighbor

The second Great Commandment urges, "Love your neighbor as yourself." Who counts as a "neighbor"? The parable of the Good Samaritan[6] suggests that our duty extends beyond the close circle of friends and family who love us in return. God calls us to love *broadly*, including strangers, foreigners, outcasts, and even our enemies.

Love meets an equally stringent test at home. There, we learn to love *deeply*, often at greater personal expense, and with better comprehension of the other's true need. The trials of married love hold unrivaled power to transform our hearts. The following examples show how acts of kindness toward your mate can be at least as strenuous — and spiritually significant — as charity to a stranger:

> Kevin cleans the messy kitchen counter left from Sherry's snack, assuming that something important must have distracted her.

In daily married life, countless favors like this one go unnoticed and unappreciated. We can hardly give ourselves much credit for such ordinary events. By contrast, we can claim heroic generosity for assisting a stranger in need, even in the absence of public acclaim or any expression of gratitude from the recipient.

> Bonnie overlooks a month-long period of crabby irritability from her husband, recognizing that it springs from worry over his father's ill health — and his own looming mortality.

Married life routinely taxes the endurance of our love. It often calls us to exercise forbearance over an extended period of time, compromising any rigid standard of fairness. We can persist in selfless giving only by cultivating real generosity of spirit. By contrast, we can perform isolated acts of charity to strangers out of duty, through a burst of willpower, in the absence of heartfelt compassion.

> Joe patiently listens to his wife's rambling complaints about her job, honoring her plea to restrain himself from offering solutions. This makes him set aside his previously unexamined need to prove himself in every test he meets.

Joe's self-discipline arises out of (more-or-less) accurate awareness of his wife's need to forego his "help," in order to build confidence in her own abilities. Both parties grow. By contrast, helping a stranger permits unchallenged projection of our own needs, often leaving both parties unchanged.

So it would seem that husbands and wives are, for each other, the closest, most readily available "neighbors" on whom to practice love. The hard part comes in striking the proper balance between loving our mates and loving ourselves.

Self-Love

American culture displays an uneasy ambivalence about self-love. On one hand, we live in a capitalistic society where greed and self-promotion are taken for granted. This baldly self-serving attitude permeates our social lives, as well. We sometimes mistrust simple kindness, wondering "What's in it for you?"

Although we honor Mother Teresa and other examples of heroic self-sacrifice, hardly anyone takes them as models. We regard them with uncomprehending awe, as objects of curiosity. Nothing could be more American than the rugged individualism expressed in "taking care of Number One." From within our own shores, we scarcely notice this aggressive self-promotion, while people of other nations regard us with a mixture of envy and contempt.

At the same time, our culture lampoons self-care as if it were narcissistic indulgence. We tease people who refuse junk food or limit their exposure to the sun: "You're still going to die of *something*." People who meditate or attend personal growth workshops are judged to be self-absorbed. "They must have too much time on their hands."

For men, especially, our culture promotes callous self-neglect. America supports self-serving, competitive striving, but discourages self-nurturing. We love neither our neighbors nor ourselves very well.

Still, "Love your neighbor as yourself" remains the most well-known ethical guideline in the Western world. Who could doubt its fundamental wisdom? But like other maxims, this one suffers from too much success. It has become so familiar that we seldom hear its full significance. We usually blink at the crucial, closing phrase, which shows *how* to love our neighbors.

Conventional Christian piety routinely slights self-love by emphasizing the duty to love our neighbors. The most severe preachers cast charitable love in opposition to self-love, confusing it with selfishness. Erich Fromm recognized this mistake long ago, in his classic book *The Art of Loving*:

> Selfishness and self-love, far from being identical, are actually opposites. The selfish person does not love himself too much but too little; in fact he hates himself.... It is true that selfish persons are incapable of loving others, but they are not capable of loving themselves either.[7]

No one can cultivate a compassionate heart through an act of the will. Self-love must serve as the model and foundation for loving anyone else. We can give of ourselves only to the extent we succeed in finding ourselves. Mature self-love represents an uncommon developmental attainment.

For a newborn, Self encompasses the entire universe. When the infant's needs are comfortably satisfied, she perceives her universal Self as Good. When she suffers deprivation or discomfort, she can only judge the entire universe (including herself) as Bad.[8] So the earliest foundation for healthy self-love rests on reasonably reliable fulfillment of the infant's needs. During the second year of life, children learn to acknowledge the semi-independent existence of other individuals. But an inflated sense of Self persists at least until age ten or twelve.

From within this egocentric perspective, children harbor delusions of omnipotent power. They imagine themselves the prime, causal agent behind all unexplained events. So when Mom gets crabby, or even when parents divorce, children tend to assume responsibility. They strive to justify whatever befalls them, loving or hating themselves, consistent with their fate. Not until adolescence do they gradually develop the cognitive power to shed these superstitions, enabling formation of a normal, separate identity. Even during the late teenage years, they have only scant comprehension of how to regard this unfolding Self, except as significant others have treated them, for better or worse.[9]

Few people manage to approach God directly to heal their wounded capacity to love themselves and their neighbors. For most of us, imperfect human love functions as a crucial stepping stone to greater love in all its forms. But how can we proceed when (1) we can love ourselves no better than our parents loved us; and (2) we can love another person no better than we can love ourselves? The outlook would appear fatalistic and discouraging, were it not for one redeeming factor: The extraordinary grace of falling in love calls attention to the empty places in our souls, and revives hopeful yearning to have them filled.

Conjugal Give-and-Take

Marriage compels us to balance self-assertion and self-sacrifice. Initially, romantic idealism inspires extravagant consideration for our partners. The illusion of merged identity blurs any distinction between what's best for me and what's best for you: "*We* are one. So nothing gives me greater satisfaction than making you happy."

When this benevolence comes at the forfeit of our own needs, though, we can't sustain it. The honeymoon ends when we can no longer deny that our needs often conflict with the needs of our mates. We start to resent their failure to mirror our generosity. We're shocked to discover how selfish and ungrateful they can be.

Many marriages falter at this crucial stage. Some sink into ugly power struggles. Some stagnate in passive alienation. Some end in divorce.

Other couples hammer out an acceptable exchange that gradually expands into free-flowing love, with no need to keep score. The difference hinges on whether we bring adequate self-love to the relationship. When our mates disappoint us, a minimal reserve of self-love bolsters assurance of our own worthiness. This prompts self-consolation, and better enables us to keep the faith that love will prevail.

Glancing through the theater section of the Sunday paper, while lingering over a second cup of coffee, Rachel comes across the listing for a play that immediately excites her interest. She likes most romantic comedies, and this one wins high praise from the reviewer. Rachel marks brackets around some key phrases, as she maps a strategy to entice her husband, Mike.

Rachel knows that he usually winces at the prospect of attending the theater. But they have seen countless films together since he last consented to a live production. She has even endured several of the action movies that he likes so much. Just last night, Mike complained of falling into a recreation rut. So Rachel hopes he will appreciate her for uncovering this fresh prospect.

Rachel finds her husband planted on the couch. Advertising images flash mutely across the TV screen, as Mike studies the Sports section of the newspaper, awaiting the start of Today's Big Game. "Good timing," Rachel thinks to herself. "I need to act fast."

"How does this sound to you?" she inquires innocently: "Uproariously funny...illuminates the subtleties of modern relationships...top-notch performances. Splendid entertainment."

Rachel's soaring optimism crashes into a mountain of stubborn resistance. "Sounds like a chick flick," Mike snorts. "You know that 'subtleties' are lost on me, Babe — especially when it comes to relationships. And I usually prefer 'harrowing' over 'splendid.'" He chuckles at his own cleverness.

Rachel can't suppress a smile either. He can muster endearing humor even when acting piggy. "I don't see why relationships should interest only women. You happen to be involved in one yourself, you know," she reminds him, trying to maintain a playful tone. "Besides that, it's not a movie. It's a play. Don't you remember saying we need to find something different to do?"

Mike groans in imitation of Eeyore. "Forty dollars a pop to watch overacting wasn't quite what I had in...Whoa! Almost missed the kickoff." He lunges for the remote control.

"I married a Philistine," Rachel mutters as she turns away in disappointment. Back in the kitchen, she slams the folded newspaper down on the counter. "Mike can be so narrow-minded and selfish sometimes," she grumbles to no one. "It's not right. I deserve better."

At half-time, Mike tracks Rachel down, finding her curled up with a book. "Hey, how ya doin'?" he asks, crowding into the overstuffed chair beside her and claiming a long, wet kiss. He's relieved that she warmly returns his affection. "Does this mean that you're not mad at me for shooting down your suggestion for some 'splendid' entertainment?"

"I was mad for a while...but I got over it."

"Thanks for letting go of that theater stuff. You know I—"

"Who said I let it go?" Rachel interrupts. "I called the box office and reserved two tickets for next Saturday night. You're invited, but if you don't want to go, just let me know in a couple days. I can find another date." She pauses to enjoy his stricken look before explaining, "I also called my friend Maxine. She said she'd love to join me if you back out."

Mike looks worried for a moment, but then smiles with grudging respect. He knows it's his move.

Under conditions of adequate self-love, marriage prompts the emergence of our best, true selves. The trials of intimate encounter help us discern our gifts and weaknesses more realistically. We carve out our preferences and values in relation to a mate who sometimes chooses differently. We learn to claim our essential freedoms and secure our personal boundaries, by fending off a partner's inevitable attempts to encroach on them. We shoulder our responsibilities in response to a partner who refuses to carry our share. We discover our inner authority by standing up to a formidable adversary ready to assume control over us.

Through this boisterous give-and-take, we find our legitimate places in creation. At one moment, marriage prods us to assert our rights. At the next, we meet a challenge to extend ourselves for the sake of our beloved.

Our mates unwittingly collaborate with God by inspiring self-improvement, and by drawing out our capacity for trust, surrender and awe. In marriage, we learn how to love our closest neighbor as ourselves. Doing so, we discover how to love God. The next chapter shows how marriage promotes thankfulness, forgiveness, humility and grace.

Three

The Virtues of Love

A wonderful marriage doesn't make life easy or painless, it just makes the work sweeter, and the pain more meaningful.—David Schnarch[1]

Married life fosters a wide range of universal spiritual values. It prompts us to cultivate traditional virtues such as thankfulness, forgiveness and humility. Above all, marriage teaches the ways of grace.

Thankfulness

Anyone paying attention notices a multitude of blessings that flow from his mate. This holds true in all but the most hateful relationships. At the simple, practical level, who cooks your meals? Who cleans the house? Who mows the lawn? Who dispatches the fearsome spiders that creep into your bedroom?

On a more personal scale, who is that familiar presence beside you when you awaken? Who listens to you when you have a problem? Who gratifies you sexually? Who comforts you when you're discouraged or afraid? Who takes care of you when you're sick? Who makes you laugh?

Perhaps your mate doesn't perform all these favors. Sometimes, no doubt, the services rendered fail to satisfy your detailed preferences. Such deficits in no way discount the value of whatever your mate provides.

For that matter, your mate deserves thanks even for her faults, insofar as they prod you to grow, in order to contend with them. The most aggravating behavior usually feels *so* intolerable because it tweaks a personal sensitivity in need of healing correction. The ability to bear these irritations lightly, recognizing them as a stimulus to your own growth, represents a mark of spiritual advancement.

A grateful heart develops with training and practice. In marriage, if you fail to adopt a thankful attitude, a self-respecting mate will find a way to prompt you.

Sam and Virginia consider themselves old-fashioned. They're modern enough to each claim an equal say in weighty decisions, like buying a car or choosing a vacation. Aside from that, they mainly adhere to traditional roles. Sam is the breadwinner, earning a modest living for the family as a forklift operator in a factory. He also does the heavy yard work, and some minor household repairs.

Virginia proudly wears the title of homemaker. In addition to cooking, cleaning and gardening, she does all the shopping, and manages the household finances. As Sam likes to joke, "I make the money. She spends it."

Neither Sam nor Virginia sees any need to express lavish thanks for the completion of routine chores. He might occasionally compliment her on a special dinner, or she might remark on his extra work to spruce up the yard in advance of hosting a barbecue. More often, their gratitude goes unspoken. They have always shown respect for each other's specialized competence by never meddling outside their own domains.

When they send the first of their children to college, the added financial burden strains these unspoken accords. It stirs feelings of inadequacy in Sam, who responds by launching an economy campaign. First, he proposes a moratorium on clothing expenditures. Virginia readily consents. Next, he suggests they could reduce their utility bill by conserving water and electricity. Virginia considers this misguided, but she tries to cooperate.

Then, one evening, she notices her husband reading the grocery store flyers. "Really, Sam, you don't need to trouble yourself," she assures him. "I always check the ads."

"Well, did you notice that Acme has a special on hamburger this week?"

"Yes, I saw that."

"So how much are you going to buy?"

"Actually, I'm not shopping at Acme this week."

"How can you pass up a bargain like this?"

"Every week, I check the ads from Acme and QwikMart. This week, QwikMart has better prices on the items we need."

"We can always use hamburger. Or put it in the freezer. At this price, I think we should get several pounds. You can still do the other shopping at QwikMart. Then, go to Acme for the hamburger."

"Give it a rest, Sam. We have plenty of hamburger in the freezer, which is nearly full already. Besides, I can't run around to every store in town, chasing one bargain here, and another there. I'd spend more in gas than the few cents I'd save — not to mention the waste of my time."

"Well, maybe I'll stop at Acme on my way home from work," Sam insists. In his penny-pinching zeal, he's exceeding the limits of Virginia's patience.

"Suit yourself. But if you bring home hamburger, you'd better plan on cooking it, too. I already had menus planned for this week." With that, Virginia turns and walks away. Sam thinks she's just acting dramatic to make her point.

The next evening, he arrives home later than usual, proudly carrying two bags from the supermarket. Virginia greets him cheerfully. "Would you like some help putting these groceries away?" she offers.

When they finish, Sam reaches for the newspaper. "How long before dinner?" he asks.

"I don't know. How are you going to cook this hamburger?"

"What do you mean?"

"Well, since you've taken over the dinner chores, I had time to start a sewing project. I'll be working in the den. Call me when dinner's ready."

That night, the family eats cheeseburger sandwiches — on plain, white bread, since Sam had purchased no buns. "I couldn't find any lettuce or tomatoes in the house, either," he explains apologetically.

"That's OK. These are fine."

After dinner, Virginia volunteers to wash dishes. Troubled by the implications of this unwanted role reversal, Sam joins in. "You know," he says, as he dries the frying pan, "I can see now that there's more involved in putting food on the table than I ever realized."

"You'll learn." Virginia won't let him off the hook too easily.

"Maybe. But I'll never catch up to your twenty-one years of experience. I was way out of line, butting into stuff that I don't know anything about. Our financial pinch has been making me crazy. I'm sorry I took it out on you, instead of giving you credit for serving up such delicious meals on our tight budget. If you'll take over again, you can count on a lot more appreciation from me."

With a little more coaxing, Virginia relents. She resumes her customary shopping and cooking duties, without further interference. Thereafter, thanks flow more freely between them, in both directions.

Marriage presents countless occasions to practice thankfulness. From grateful acknowledgment of the favors bestowed by your mate, it's only a short step to thanking God for creating this extraordinary creature as your partner and helpmate.

Forgiveness

Above all others, our mates know how to hurt us. They see our most carefully guarded frailties, and have access to us in our most vulnerable moments. They also have motive to inflict pain: deliberately, in defending their own tender parts by means of preemptive attack; or carelessly, in pursuing their own agendas without regard for someone so easily taken for granted.

The danger expands with growing investment in the relationship. The more you care about your mate's opinion, the more it hurts when she turns on you. Ironically, the stronger the marriage, the greater our vulnerability to each other. And so, in marriage, we confront the most profound challenges of forgiveness, with the highest stakes hanging in the balance.

Ordinarily, the power of forgiveness is best reserved for major offenses, such as disloyalty, betrayal or cruelty. However, chronic repetition can amplify a small slight until it reaches proportions that you cannot, and should not, ignore. Or worse, if your mate persists in some action just because it galls you, then it becomes a gesture of contempt — a cowardly way of inflicting emotional pain without risking a direct, frontal attack. Never let generous forbearance lapse into tolerance for mistreatment.

In other relationships, you might settle for unilateral forgiveness — letting go of resentment for the sake of lightening your heart, and then retreating beyond the range of further harm. But a lifetime commitment makes it essential to pursue the deeper healing of reconciliation. To achieve reconciliation, you must secure collaboration from the offender, in the form of empathy, sincere regret and convincing assurance of intent to avoid repeating the injustice. Such deep contrition comes hard. Your partner may even refuse to acknowledge having committed a significant misdeed. In that case, you must translate your complaint into terms that capture your mate's attention.

Jim knows he's in trouble as soon as he turns into the parking lot for the building where his wife works. Betty stands stiffly by the curb, waiting for him. Even from thirty yards away, he can see that she's mad. A glance at his watch confirms why: twenty minutes late...again. He kept her waiting at least that long every day last week. So he can't really blame her for being upset that he's starting a new week the same way. He just hopes she'll get over it quickly.

"Sorry I'm late," Jim offers lamely, as she gets in the passenger seat. Betty makes no reply. During the tense silence that follows, Jim mulls over the events leading up to this moment.

First, he reviews the preceding hour, sifting for a credible excuse. Just before quitting time, Jim tried to fit one last call into his workday. "This guy's never in his office, so I'll just leave a quick message," he rationalized. Then the client answered in person, and the call ran long.

Jim decides against trying to explain all this to Betty. She's tired of his excuses. He's tired of trying to justify himself. The circumstances always seem compelling to him, but deep down, he knows that nothing warrants such habitual lack of consideration.

The problem began ten days ago, when their second car broke down. Unable to afford the repair until their tax refund arrives, they decided to carpool, since their offices are only a mile apart. Jim needs the car for business errands, so he will drop Betty off in the morning, and pick her up after work.

On their first day of carpooling, Jim hurried to put the finishing touches on a sales report before leaving the office. It took longer than expected. Before he could even explain this to Betty, she graciously shrugged off the inconvenience. "Don't worry about it. These things happen."

Nor did she complain when he showed up late again the next day. "Maybe he got caught in a traffic jam," she thought, giving her husband the benefit of the doubt. Jim neglected to mention that he had he simply lost track of time while kidding around with his buddies.

On Wednesday, he made a trip to the hardware store before meeting Betty. This time, she spoke up: "Don't you realize how miserable it is for me, standing here on tired feet, breathing exhaust fumes for half an hour while I wait for you? It gets embarrassing, waving to all my coworkers as they drive away."

"Sorry, Honey. I'll try to do better."

"I thought you had been trying all along. If this is the best you can do, we need to come up with a new arrangement."

"That won't be necessary. I'll pick you up on time tomorrow, for certain."

When he failed to do so, arriving twenty-five minutes late, Betty was steaming. This time, Jim foolishly defended himself, minimizing her complaint.

"What's the big deal? So I'm a few minutes late. You can't expect me to watch the clock continuously when I'm so busy." This cavalier attitude only compounded Betty's anger.

Jim's pattern continued on Friday. But little did he realize, Betty was using her time at the curb to do some serious thinking about her predicament. "I refuse to go on like this," she had declared, as she climbed into the car.

Just as Jim recalls this warning, the sound of Betty clearing her throat interrupts his reverie. "Here it comes," he thinks to himself, dreading the expected onslaught.

So he's shocked when she calmly announces, "You won't have to pick me up from work tomorrow."

"So you're getting a ride with a friend?"

"No. I'm going to call a taxi."

"Don't be ridiculous. We can't afford that!"

"I know. But I refuse to end every workday getting upset waiting for you."

"I didn't realize you were so bent out of shape over this," Jim says. "Won't you forgive me?"

"Actually, I'm not angry anymore. On Friday, I was furious. All through the weekend, I kept trying to shake it off, struggling to forgive you. Then, I realized forgiving didn't make sense, when the same thing kept happening. So I decided the next time you left me waiting, I'd make sure it was the last time. *Now* I can forgive you."

Betty's unruffled clarity confuses Jim. "So does that mean you won't have to follow through on your threat to take a taxi?"

"Not at all. I can forgive you *because* I'm taking a taxi home tomorrow."

"That's not fair," Jim complains. "You're just punishing me."

"No, I'm making my problem *our* problem."

"I'll do better. Don't you trust me?"

Betty laughs. "Are you kidding? I trust you in other ways, but it's obvious I can't rely on you to pick me up on time."

Jim doesn't like this turn of events. But he likes it better than enduring a scolding and feeling guilty. Later that evening, he offers a convincing apology. Betty accepts it, but still holds firm to her plan.

For the next three days, she takes a cab home. On Friday morning, Jim makes a proposal: "With the money you'd spend on a cab this afternoon, we could catch an early movie. How about if I pick you up at five o'clock sharp?" After considering for a moment, Betty agrees. Jim arrives exactly on time.

Forgiveness forges strength out of vulnerability. It calls us to feel our hurt and resentment to the point of determination to heal them. It expresses faith that love can prevail over injustice. These principles of forgiveness are taught nowhere else so clearly and forcefully as in marriage.

Humility

All spirituality must contend with ego. The ego sets itself up as a demigod, separate from everyone else, continually striving for privilege and power. This denies our paradoxical human condition: simultaneously humble *and* exalted, autonomous *and* dependent. In the quest to win special status and privilege, the ego forfeits the universal spiritual ideal of community, in alliance with God.

Every religion devises strategies for taming the ego. The most primitive approach aims to subdue it directly, through austerities like fasting, or long periods of kneeling in prayer on a stone floor. Physical ordeals often backfire, though. As much as the ego relishes pleasure, it takes pride in heroic accomplishment. So the more severe the privation, the more readily the ego claims prestige.

Indirect methods achieve better results. Charitable service, for example, distracts the ego from self-preoccupation by confronting us with the suffering of others. Still the ego may persist in grasping for glory, trying to distinguish itself by outperforming other volunteers, in a kind of spiritual materialism. Ultimately, all the traditional, religious disciplines are merely vehicles for traveling the spiritual pathway. They do not necessarily take us to God. With the ego driving, they can as easily carry us down meaningless detours or into a ditch.

Marriage is uniquely well-suited to keeping the ego in check. We unwittingly select a partner who's able to serve as our own foil. Whenever we unreasonably insist that we're right, our mates marshal evidence to prove us wrong. Whenever we puff ourselves up to unrealistic proportions, our mates step forward to puncture our conceit. By methods fair or foul, direct or devious, potent or passive, our mates usually find the perfect way to thwart our pursuit of selfish advantage.

Even as a child, Amy's good looks attracted special attention and privilege. Now, at age twenty-nine, she possesses the kind of otherworldly beauty that stops men in their tracks. Most of them merely stare. The bolder ones scramble to perform some favor, hoping to bask in her radiance a little longer.

While Amy insists that she does nothing to exploit this power, she's accustomed to men falling over each other to open doors for her. She accepts it as the natural order — sometimes embarrassing and intrusive, but often very convenient, especially in her career selling expensive, high-tech office machines to large corporations. Male purchasing agents seldom decline her request for a second appointment to demonstrate her company's latest product line.

Four years ago, Amy met Neil in the course of her work. He was a fast-rising young executive whose assent she needed to close a big sale. After the successful completion of their negotiations, Neil suggested dinner together, to celebrate. They both felt the powerful chemistry between them, but they were cautious about the dangers of mixing business with a personal relationship. So they let their romance develop at a discreet pace.

Amy appreciates Neil's self-assured composure. He is the first man she ever dated who isn't awestruck by her. Although only average-looking, he is, like Amy, comfortable wielding power. He treats her with respect and consideration, but he has nothing to prove and no one to impress.

Soon after their marriage, two years ago, Amy began to notice the drawbacks of living with someone who doesn't always cater to her. Neil is impeccably fair about doing his share of the household chores, but to him, everything is open to negotiation.

When their new dog throws up in the house for the first time, Amy is dismayed that Neil does not rush to clean it up. For a few moments, they just stare at the mess on their carpet. Then, they both back away.

"That looks really disgusting," Neil says, turning his head aside. "Whew! Smells bad, too."

"It's gross," Amy agrees. "Well... aren't you going to clean it up?"

"Somebody's going to have to do it," Neil says noncommittally. "...and soon, too, before that becomes a permanent stain."

"Not me."

"Wait a minute. I don't remember volunteering. Besides, I've done most of the dirty work ever since we've been married. Who always disposes of the refrigerator science projects? Who scraped the dead possum off the pavement in front of our house? Who mopped the bathroom floor when the toilet overflowed? Don't you think it's about your turn?"

Amy glances at the steaming mess on their rug and shudders at the thought of approaching it. "I, I... I guess you're right. It's only fair. But I feel sick already. I don't think I can."

"Of course you *can*. You mean you just don't *want* to," Neil says firmly. "You lived on your own in an apartment for several years. You must have confronted a few disgusting chores."

"Well, I do remember a time when I opened the door one morning, and an alley cat streaked inside, carrying a mouse — a really big one, almost like a rat. I tried to chase the cat back outside, but he ran under my bed. Then I heard these gruesome crunching sounds. When he finally emerged, licking his chops, I peeked under the bed and glimpsed a gory, half-eaten carcass."

"So, you cleaned it up, right? You didn't just leave it to rot, did you?"

"I shrieked and ran outside. This nice guy who lived next door rushed out to see what was the matter. Since I was so upset, *he* offered to clean it up."

"Well, I'm not as nice a guy as your former neighbor. I'm not going to clean up *every* vile mess. I don't like it any better than you do." Then, shaking his head, trying to suppress a smile, Neil continues in a softer tone. "I can see that this is going to be a big adjustment for you. So I'll take care of this one. But the next time Sparky gets indigestion, you'd better be ready."

"Maybe we should reconsider pet ownership. I didn't realize all the duties."

Neil turns to address the dog. "Did you hear that? Now you know who really loves you."

"I didn't mean it, Sparky," Amy insists. Then, haltingly, she begins to prepare herself for the day she dreads. "I'll get some rubber gloves...and maybe a surgical mask...."

As a child, Amy was blessed to learn that she is special. Gradually, she came to understand both the advantages *and* the liabilities of her lofty status. She was drawn to Neil because he treated her like an ordinary person, instead of a princess. Here, she discovers that ordinary people must contend with some disagreeable realities.

Marriage humbles us at every turn. Monogamous sexuality especially defies the ego. We can hardly feign self-sufficiency in the midst of burning sexual hunger. Compelling desire prompts outreach to a partner who has already seen our best seductive moves.

Furthermore, over the course of a long marriage, everyone suffers lapses in sexual desire and performance, undermining any superhuman claim to the title of Sex Machine.

Our mates also teach us humility by frustrating any attempt to change them. Whenever we imagine we could improve upon their appearance, conduct or attitude, they help us see the folly of our presumption. Typically, they redirect our attention to how we ought to change ourselves.

Grace

When our mates offer unearned love, they invite a different kind of submission by the ego. Grace strips away false pride. When we permit someone to love us unconditionally, to provide for us in our need, and to cherish us beyond the reach of our merit, the ego has no ground on which to stand. Such occasions of grace remind us of our fundamental identity as children of God: We are flawed creatures, nonetheless loved and blessed. Marriage partners can best illuminate this lesson for each other.

Ordinarily, in the competitive world, we guard against exposing any weakness, lest someone take advantage. Success depends on making a favorable impression. So in the workplace, and even socially, we dread getting caught in a mistake.

Different standards apply in marriage. This is not to suggest that carelessness, complacent underachievement, or inconsiderate conduct will be better tolerated. Marriage partners, even more than employers, expect a good faith effort. But over the long haul of living together, we come to recognize the sheer folly of trying to *earn* love on the merit of exceptional qualities and outstanding performance. Living in such close proximity, our faults and weaknesses leak out again and again, forcing us to come to terms with our limitations. At best, we discover that the flow of love from our mates continues undiminished in the wake of failure.

Duane takes pride in his careful attention to detail. He always presents an impeccably neat appearance; he adheres to strict standards of punctuality; he finds comfort in having rules to guide his conduct. Most people perceive him as stiff and humorless, but his compulsive tendencies serve him well in his job as a quality control inspector with an electronics manufacturing firm. After ten years there, his conscientious service finally earns a promotion.

As a supervisor, Duane performs less effectively. He prowls the production line, ready to pounce on the slightest irregularity. This harsh, nit-picking style soon alienates his subordinates, who constantly mock him. Morale and production decline under his leadership.

Not long after Duane's promotion, he marries for the first time, at age forty-one. His bride, Norma, is a sweet young woman, fifteen years his junior, and far behind him in education as well. They are peers in one regard: neither has much experience dating.

For eight years following the death of her mother, Norma served as a full-time, live-in caretaker for her invalid father. Duane often saw her at church, dutifully positioned at her father's side, in the area designated for wheelchairs. But they never spoke, until one Sunday she showed up alone, and the usher happened to direct her to a vacant seat beside Duane.

After the service, Duane expressed his condolences on the death of her father, which had been announced from the pulpit. They struck up an easy conversation. Six months later, Duane proposed.

Duane adores Norma, and she admires his apparent maturity and competence. In sharp contrast to his stern workplace demeanor, Duane treats his wife with remarkable tenderness.

He showers her with compliments. He's quick to draw her a bath or massage her shoulders. He enjoys indulging her with flowers and small gifts. With Norma, he feels strong and expansive, like a prince. Elsewhere, he feels small and tight and anxious.

Duane's devotion to Norma does not prevent him from correcting her behavior, in everything from her grammar to her driving habits. But he always addresses her in the gentlest possible way, as a doting parent might instruct a child. The church gossips judge Duane's conduct as patronizing. "He treats her like a pet," one sniped, after observing him dish food onto Norma's plate at a potluck. But Norma seldom takes offense at Duane's paternalistic attitude. She counts herself lucky to have such a fine gentleman lavishing attention on her.

This congenial picture clouds over when Duane is suddenly fired from his job. Devastated, he can't bring himself to confess such a humiliating setback. So he arises each morning at the customary hour of five, eats his usual breakfast, kisses Norma good-bye and drives away, as if to work.

In the mornings, he scours the Help Wanted ads, hoping to quickly find a comparable new position, and avoid telling Norma about getting fired until after regaining his dignity. Afternoons are spent sitting on a park bench, wringing his hands in anxious despair. At home in the evenings, Norma wonders about her husband's dispirited mood, despite his feeble pretense that everything is fine.

Money is no immediate concern. Duane saved enough during his bachelor days to cover expenses for a year or more. He simply feels ashamed. Believing he won Norma on his merit as a reliable provider and protector, he fears that in losing his job, he forfeits her respect.

When Duane finally admits the truth, after maintaining his charade for a week, Norma first responds with outrage.

"How could you withhold something so important? This affects both of us. Do you think I can't handle bad news? Well, you underestimate me — and what I went through, taking care of my father. You may enjoy treating me like your little girl, and until now, it seemed harmless enough. But I'm not a child. I signed on as your partner in life. Did it never occur to you that I might be able to help?"

"It's none of that. I just couldn't face you. I feel so worthless. It's like I've been exposed as a fraud. I was afraid ... afraid you wouldn't love me anymore." Having voiced his greatest terror, Duane breaks down.

Using both hands, Norma gently lifts his head, forcing him to meet her gaze. "Don't you know it's *you* I love? Not your accomplishments."

It will take Duane a long time to grasp the full force of this revolutionary idea. But for one lucid moment, he knows the power of grace. For the first time in memory, he feels secure.

Thus, in marriage, we stumble upon countless occasions for grace. We cannot hide our faults and weaknesses amidst the forced familiarity of long-term, daily life together. And yet, despite our apparent failings, our mates usually insist that we're nonetheless worthy of love — more on account of who we are than what we do. This, of course, mirrors the way God loves us: totally and unconditionally.

Marriage teaches thankfulness, forgiveness, humility and grace. As the examples have shown, these opportunities do not depend on pious intent. More often, our mates force recognition of a spiritual lesson in the natural course of protecting their own interests, and upholding their own self-respect. In the next chapter, you will see how *The Sacred Dance* provides all the necessary conditions for a spiritual vocation.

Four

One Flesh
Marriage as Spiritual Vocation

. . . a man leaves his father and his mother and cleaves to his wife, and they become one flesh. —Genesis 2:24

Marriage provides ideal conditions for *spiritual vocation*: a disciplined way of life that prompts spiritual awakening. Compared to the prevailing model of individual spirituality, marriage offers two main advantages: (1) An intimate observer continually calls us to self-awareness and integrity; and (2) compelling bodily experience keeps us grounded in reality. Capitalizing on this potential requires an active choice. Every couple implicitly negotiates, "What kind of marriage are we going to have?"

Spiritual Vocation

Webster defines *vocation* as "a call, summons or impulsion to perform a certain function, or enter a certain career, especially a religious one."[1] It evokes an era when most people took it for granted that God calls each of us to follow a specific life path.

According to this perspective on life, God endows every human being with a unique set of talents, inclinations and circumstances. These dispositions point us toward particular work and living arrangements. They represent our destiny, not as preordained fate, but simply an invitation to life. In taking up the discipline of spiritual vocation, we accept God's gift of life, and affirm our readiness to express God's will. Pursuing our vocation, we find joy in fulfilling our potential.

The search for a personal vocation questions our relationships as much as our career choice. A celibate vocation renounces the potential delights and complications of married love, in order to concentrate on prayer and service. This option sidesteps romantic illusions, and the worldly responsibilities of marriage. But celibacy demands heroic sacrifices, going against our instincts for intimate partnership, sexual intercourse and parenthood.

Most people choose marriage. Here, spiritual insight comes through deep intimacy and committed devotion between two people. On the surface, this may seem a less rigorous vocation than celibacy, since couples enjoy all the satisfactions of family life. Yet, a commitment to one person imposes some rigorous disciplines.

First, wedding vows exact our consent to "forsake all others," renouncing any competition. Marriage also incorporates a no-escape clause: "...'til death do you part." Confined together with our mates in this arrangement, we chafe against each other until we are rubbed raw, our defenses worn through. If we pay attention, we can hardly fail to apprehend some spiritual lessons in this emotional pressure cooker.

Marriage dictates the additional duty to respond to each other's personal needs, not to mention the needs of any children that might be born. We are bound to contribute (directly or indirectly) to the family's material support. We make ourselves accountable to each other —not slavishly, but simply as a matter of respect, caring about our mate's opinion, and taking it seriously. We must discover how to accommodate each other, while remaining true to ourselves.

One contemporary theologian describes the potential for "conjugal spirituality" this way: "Two become one temple for the spirit by continually reaching out, dedicating time, space, and energy to comprehend the presence of God which is in the other.... [The vital observances include] dialogue and sex, the prayer in action of daily encounter, periodic stocktaking and regular celebration."[2]

Celibate Bias in the Christian Tradition

Christianity provides little practical guidance for couples hoping to find a spiritual vocation in marriage. Mainstream Christian spirituality — both Catholic and Protestant — emphasizes an individual path to God. Particular denominations adhere to either the model of a monastic "group-together-with-God," or the "one-alone-with-God" practices of the hermit.[3] They overlook the realities of married life, neglecting the spiritual needs of couples, and implicitly discounting their spiritual potential.

The celibate bias of Christianity is apparent also in the lives of the saints, hardly any of whom were married. The few who wed (including America's own St. Elizabeth Anne Seton) are recognized for portions of their lives spent as single persons. None was canonized mainly on account of exemplary virtues expressed in marriage.

In the last thirty years, a trickle of published literature on conjugal spirituality has begun to appear. It amounts to very little, compared to the endless stream of material dealing with individual practice. Only the Marriage Encounter movement tries to capitalize on the unique potential of conjugal vocation. Such neglect of married spirituality falsely insinuates that this is a less ambitious pathway than religious life, or even that God and spouse are somehow in competition. Certainly, many couples make these inferences, adopting a self-image of spiritual underachievement.

A few obscure threads trace the acknowledgment of married spirituality back through centuries of Western theology.[4] As early as 155 C.E., Synesius of Cyrene resisted pressure to separate from his wife before assuming the office of bishop, arguing that it would amount to "impiety." Aelred of Rievaulx (1110–1167) recognized sex as a form of contemplation. The nineteenth-century Russian theologian Vladimir Soloviev taught that sexual love promotes unparalleled spiritual progress by enabling transcendence of the ego.

The renowned Jewish philosopher Martin Buber identified the intimate, respectful "I-thou" relationship as the primary spiritual reality. Marriage presents the best opportunity to forge this type of bond. When we set aside all preconceptions to notice the real person, we see as God sees, with understanding and compassion. In showing devotion to our mates, we indirectly express devotion to God.

Advantages of the Vocation of Marriage

Compared to individual spirituality, marriage is a more balanced vocation, less prone to delusion, because two vital factors anchor the participants in reality. First, we benefit from the presence of an intimate observer who calls us to account. If you behave selfishly, arrogantly or deceitfully, your mate will recognize it and say so. You'll be notified whenever you're judgmental, vain, crabby or ungrateful.

Living alone, we could easily rationalize our character flaws. We might succeed in concealing them even from our friends. But we cannot fool our mates. They know us too well. Equipped with this intimate knowledge, and unwilling to settle for less than our best, our mates continually prod us to hone our integrity.

Of course, you can subvert this corrective mechanism by disregarding your partner's opinion. Persisting in defensiveness, you might eventually stifle most criticism. Or you can intimidate your partner into silence by counterattacking whenever she dares to reproach you.

More legitimately, we can question how our mates' own blind spots and self-serving interests distort their perceptions. They cannot give objective advice. Still, they know us far better than any trained therapist or spiritual director ever could. Their criticisms usually have some valid basis, even when couched in unfair terms. If you want to know the truth about yourself, you have no better source than your mate.

A second factor also keeps us firmly grounded: For married couples, the spiritual drama unfolds in flesh and blood. The biblical metaphor of *one flesh* highlights the significance of uniting our *embodied* souls: "Love one another as you love your own bodies."[5] Beginning in the Middle Ages and continuing until the eighteenth century, brides and grooms in Christian ceremonies promised, *"with my body, I thee worship."*

Our perceptions of reality are subject to distortion. Our emotions are notoriously fickle. Our thoughts routinely topple into confusion. But our bodies seldom lie. We cannot discount insistent bodily urgings. Physical sensations of pain and pleasure, desire and satisfaction, strike with undeniable immediacy. They are irrepressible, except through years of self-hating disregard.

Among all our bodily experiences, sex holds special potential for discovering the sacred amidst mundane physical existence. Sexual ecstasy profoundly alters our consciousness, suspending time, unhinging the ego, and opening the heart. It invites comparison to mystical states. In sex, we encounter unique opportunities for negotiating spiritually charged issues like trust, surrender and shame.

Carnal knowledge is no mere euphemism. During sexual intercourse, lovers are sometimes flooded with vast, ineffable realizations about themselves, their relationship to each other and to God. Such rapture especially visits those who intentionally dedicate themselves to creating a joint temple for Spirit. In marriage, the body, more than the mind, serves as the conduit of revelation.

The spiritual potential of our bodies extends well beyond the sexual arena. In the daily routines of married life, we see spiritual truths written on slates of flesh. The glory of creation is nowhere more evident than in your mate's body. Marriage entitles us to look closely, and see each other thoroughly. The customary prohibitions don't apply. We can stare if we want.

On the dark side, aging and illness testify to the impermanence of the physical world. We tend to minimize the decline of our own bodies — or feel overwhelmed by it. Etiquette (as much as vanity) makes us shield our infirmities, even from close friends. But marriage partners give poignant witness to the ravages of time and disease, prompting compassion, and highlighting the precious transience of embodied life.

A Brief History of Marriage

Considering the apparent spiritual potential of marriage, why do so few couples succeed in combining spiritual ambition with sexual passion and friendship, all under the umbrella of lifelong marriage? Until the current era, at least one element was usually reckoned incompatible with the others. Traditional cultures seldom recognized spontaneous mutual attraction as a valid basis for marriage. Families arranged marriages according to economic and political motives. Marriage served to cement alliances between clans, socialize children, and establish lineage for property inheritance. Society strictly defined and enforced conjugal roles.

Until the Industrial Revolution, marriage was much more intricately woven into the broader social fabric, supported by extended family and local community. That does not mean that couples received support in seeking personal fulfillment through marriage. This concern, so predominant in our era, could hardly have registered alongside the pressing requirements of duty and bare survival. Partners in marriage counted themselves lucky to achieve marginal compatibility. No one expected sexual ardor to prevail, and spirituality was typically a matter for the assembly of men. History provides a few notable variations on this arrangement.

In ancient China, Taoist philosophers elaborated detailed sexual practices believed to promote both physical and spiritual well-being. Harmonious coexistence was valued more generally in the household, as well. Men and women typically had little contact, though, except at mealtime and in the bedchamber. Furthermore, the woman's station was distinctly inferior, so peer relationship would have been rare.

Likewise, in ancient India, sexuality was a respectable topic of interest, with spiritual implications, especially for upper-class men. Around the fourth century, a sage compiled the *Kama Sutra*. This famous manual of sex and love classifies myriad types of caresses, kisses, athletic sexual positions, and strategies of seduction, in a curious mix of sentimentality and pragmatism. India is also home to the sexual cult of Tantra. But the mystical union sought in Tantra was considered unlikely between husband and wife, so participating couples usually exchanged partners.

The Hebrews have always recognized marriage as sacred. Beginning with the prophets Hosea and Jeremiah, marriage was taken to symbolize the Covenant between God and the people of Israel.[6] Jewish culture also expressed an earthy appreciation for married sexuality, counting it among the good gifts of God. The Talmud even declared it a husband's duty to see that his wife is sexually satisfied. Still, this was a fiercely patriarchal society in biblical times. Wives possessed few rights. A husband could cast off his wife if she displeased him in any way — or even if another simply pleased him more — merely by putting his intention in writing. Divorced women were dishonored and generally shunned. Lacking the support of a man, they often had no recourse but prostitution. So the threat of divorce kept women duly submissive.

Jesus opposed this injustice. He called for a spirit of unity in marriage, teaching that a man should not divorce his wife for *any* cause, except perhaps unfaithfulness. According to the gospel of John (2:1–11) Jesus performed his first miracle at a wedding in Cana. The act of changing water into wine suggests that marriage transforms mundane existence into something spiritual and inspirational. Against prevailing custom, Jesus showed women the same respect as men. Following his example, the earliest Christian communities granted women exceptional freedom and dignity, far exceeding the modest trend already underway in the broader Greco-Roman society.

The church soon overturned this progressive legacy. The Apostle Paul's preference for celibacy fit neatly with the prevailing ascetic ideals of Greek Stoic philosophy, which exerted strong influence over Christianity during the formative, early centuries. The Gnostics and other popular Christian splinter groups condemned sexuality as evil, and discouraged marriage. Although the mainstream defenders of marriage prevailed, most of them conceded the spiritual superiority of celibacy. They argued that couples should limit sexual intercourse to procreative purposes, to avoid enslavement to pleasure.[7] Following Paul more than Jesus on this point, Christianity has displayed a distinct ambivalence toward marriage.

All of our modern, Western notions of romance arise from the cult of courtly love which sprang up in southern France during the twelfth century. During that era, many knights and other prominent men traveled far from home, for years at a time, on Crusades to the Holy Land. To amuse the wealthy wives left behind, troubadours devised an intriguing literary theme that was soon imitated in real life: A man esteems a high-ranking lady of impeccable virtue and inspirational beauty; he aspires to win her attention and become worthy of her through heroic deeds and romantic gallantry, until at last, she falls in love with him.

In theory, this "ennobling love" ruled out sexual consummation. Such crass indulgence would tarnish the lady's virtue. So a veneer of spiritual aspiration, in the form of chivalrous restraint, overlaid the romantic story line. Marriage was out of the question, even if the woman were not already committed, because people believed the duties incumbent on spouses contradicted the courtly premise of *freely given* love.

Upper-class Victorian England was the first society that ever seriously tried to impose marriage upon romance. This ambition tested the limits of earnest British determination. Couples discovered they could maintain a romantically idealized image of each other only at the expense of sexual passion. Men were conveniently able to shift their sexual focus to "disreputable" women. Prostitution consequently flourished in the nineteenth century, not only in the British Empire, but all throughout Europe and America, wherever Victorian attitudes gained currency.[8] "Decent" Christian women were expected to feel neither desire nor sexual pleasure. This categorization of women as either whores or madonnas still haunts contemporary Western society.

The spiritual potential of marriage has gained wider recognition only in the last few decades.[9] This mounting interest awaited modern secular developments such as (1) a dramatic increase in longevity, resulting in far more couples living together fifty years or more; (2) improvement in the economic and social status of women, so that marriage has become increasingly a matter of choice; (3) publication of popular psychology self-help books, providing the concepts and language necessary for couples to discuss their relationships; and (4) a parallel increase in public knowledge and openness about sexuality.

Other Varieties of Marriage

If the spiritual vocation of marriage suits your temperament and values, it holds unrivaled potential to fulfill human nature. Still, it is only one of several marital options. Alternatives abound in our pluralistic culture — more than at any other time or place in history. All couples benefit from clarifying their vision for marriage. The following categories illustrate the range of possibilities currently practiced in America.

Dramatic marriage

Dramatic marriages are driven by vague, desperate neediness. Neither party is capable of the self-examination needed to achieve harmony, let alone spiritual discernment. Instead, they try to extort proof of "love," by way of coercion and florid emotional displays. Most of these demands go unfulfilled, causing relentless conflict, blaming and retaliation.

Jealousy is a chief concern for these couples. Out of insecurity, they constantly strive to control each other. The threat of violence often lurks beneath the surface.

These soap opera relationships can be surprisingly durable. The participants thrive on the excitement. Some take perverse pride in the emotional heat they generate—which sometimes ignites passionate sex. But the thrills seldom outweigh the misery. One spouse may achieve the transient satisfaction of exerting power over the other, but victor and victim are held securely in the same trap.

Authoritarian marriage

In this arrangement, couples try to make their marriage conform to a strict standard, like Procrustes, the mythical Greek giant who stretched his captives or trimmed their legs to make them fit the beds he provided. The standards for marriage might derive from cultural traditions, popular psychology or even religious dogma.

Problems arise when a couple defers to any authoritative source for the solution to practical conflicts. The circumstances of marriage are so complex, and the participants so varied, no set of regulations could possibly govern every important contingency. If the rules are few, they are too vague to provide useful guidance. If the rules are many, which one takes priority in a particular case? Striving to uphold some dogmatic formula, couples must suppress legitimate issues that could otherwise illuminate the transformative workings of love.

As long as both parties adhere to the same belief system, they may sidestep open controversy for a while, taking comfort in the apparent security that comes with having clear-cut roles and rules to follow. That dubious sense of security comes at the expense of vitality, intimacy and growth. At best, these couples forfeit many opportunities for spiritual development. Marriage becomes one more arena of barren conformity. Worse, such rules are conducive to abuse. The more dominant spouse commonly rationalizes the demands of ego in the name of obedience to doctrine.

Convenience marriage

Some couples maintain merely a practical affiliation, with little or no attention to cultivating deeper alliance. They often observe a sharp division of labor: One spouse, usually the wife, specializes in parenting and keeping a comfortable home; in return, the husband pursues an outside career, providing financial support for the family. Beyond this exchange of services, they lead separate lives, with independent interests and friends. The unspoken agreement may include even tolerance for discreet affairs.

Many business people, professionals, politicians, and career military choose this option. There is nothing inherently wrong with it. In practice, however, it commonly defrauds and exploits the economically dependent partner, who assumed a mutual willingness to enter into wider partnership. If the power imbalance is not too great, these marriages can exist with integrity, as long as both partners find satisfaction in their careers, and adequate support from other people.

The modest expectations of convenience marriage may reflect low self-worth in one or both of the participants. Keeping busy, they don't notice the accumulation of unmet needs and resentment. Then, upon retirement, these feelings often erupt in crisis, or merely simmer in depression.

Limited partnership

Limited partnership involves a deep, conscious alliance in some arenas, but not others. A couple may actively collaborate in parenting, decision-making and simple companionship, while systematically neglecting other potentials — like sexuality and emotional intimacy. This is the typical American lifestyle. Many couples begin marriage with vague hopes for a deeper union, but soon reach a stalemate. After repeatedly bumping up against the same, painful obstacle, with no apparent prospect of resolution, they tacitly agree it isn't worth the aggravation to pursue the matter any further. They may also dread the risk of divorce if they were to press their dissatisfactions too far. So they settle for what they have — which may be quite good within its boundaries.

> "He's a good provider and a decent father. He seems to respect and appreciate me, and he doesn't interfere with how I run the household. I've come to accept that he's a very private man. He doesn't like to talk about what's going on inside, and he doesn't show much interest in me personally. But nobody's perfect. We have a good marriage."

Other couples draw the lines differently:

> "We knew up front that both of us were dedicated to our careers. We understood that we'd often be apart. But we love each other. When we're together, we get along fine. Some

people say we're more like roommates. Maybe so, but she's a *really good* roommate, and we have great sex."

Who could quibble with these appraisals? Actually, many self-help authors find fault with such arrangements. They stir up insecurity with assertions that every couple *should* express their deepest feelings, *should* spend more time together, *should* grasp for complete fulfillment. These preconceived expectations ignore legitimate diversity, unfairly disparaging many couples who expressly disavow any spiritual ambition. The insistence that "one size fits all" obscures the unique spiritual opportunity awaiting couples who are prepared to observe the necessary disciplines.

No one can accomplish everything that might seem worthwhile. Some career commitments are so consuming that little time or emotional energy remains for family life. Habitual twelve-hour days at the office or frequent nights on the road are incompatible with the vocation of marriage. Certain occupations require the cultivation of attitudes antagonistic to marital intimacy.

Even within the common, modern arrangement where both husband and wife work outside the home, couples must stretch to sustain their spiritual lives together. Life demands choices. What do you choose for your marriage?

Marriage offers unparalleled opportunities for spiritual awakening, with two distinct advantages that keep us firmly grounded in reality. First, an intimate observer continually calls us to self-awareness and integrity; second, in marriage, many spiritual lessons are discerned by way of our *bodies*. Letting our partners truly *see* us — as we are exposed in sex, aging and the routine physical limitations of everyday life — we're prompted to engage spiritually charged issues like surrender, the marvel of Creation, and especially shame.

We live in an era of unprecedented, favorable conditions to practice marriage as a spiritual vocation. Yet, these benefits of marriage do not automatically accrue. In order to capitalize on the spiritual potentials surveyed here in Part One, couples must come equipped with a few, basic qualifications. These Qualifications are the subject of Part Two.

Part Two
Qualifications

To those who have, more will be given until they have an abundance. — Matthew 13:12[1]

Five key attitudes bolster a desire to tap the spiritual potential of marriage: (1) self-commitment, (2) wholesome shame, (3) desire to live a shared life, (4) tolerance for conflict, and (5) appreciation for mystery and paradox. These qualifications are vital to the vocation of marriage, just as certain building materials and tools — like wood and nails, hammer and saw — are essential to constructing a house. You might erect a marginal shelter without them. But properly equipped, you could fashion something far more cozy and substantial.

These qualifications are not severe. They are easily reframed in terms of simple willingness. Ask yourself the following questions:

1. Am I willing to live consciously, claiming personal responsibility for my life?
2. Am I willing to admit my limitations, my need for change and for help?

3. Am I willing to ardently pursue deeper knowledge of my mate, and likewise open my heart for inspection?
4. Am I willing to bear the strain of conflict?
5. Am I willing to cherish what I cannot fully understand or control?

Do some of these questions make you uneasy? This section of the book will help clarify any reservations you might feel, and open the way to new decisions that could revolutionize your marriage and your spiritual life.

Don't get discouraged if you identify yourself — or your partner — as poorly developed in one or more of the qualifications. While it's unnerving to discover a personal deficit, it's better than grappling with a nameless demon in the dark. Meager qualifications are often at the root of recurrent marital disappointments. Understanding the cause gives reason for hope. Furthermore, anyone who acknowledges an insufficiency has already taken the first step toward correcting it.

The next step calls for careful self-observation. Suppose, for example, you recognize a tendency to discount mystery and paradox. Simply pay attention to when and how you do this. (If you dare, invite your mate to help.) Notice any misgivings that arise as you try to adjust your attitude. What memories are evoked?

Then, try out the practical suggestions contained in the chapters ahead. Qualifications are tested in action. You can instantly prove your credentials by way of demonstration. Just do it, and see what happens.

Also keep in mind that these qualifications are not all-or-none features — like blue eyes — that you either possess or lack. They are dimensional — like wisdom and compassion — allowing for lifelong development. Everyone has room to grow. Ultimately, "nobody's ready for marriage. Marriage makes you ready for marriage."[2]

For anyone who is unmarried, the qualifications presented here in Part Two suggest criteria for selecting a suitable partner to join you in the Sacred Dance. But caution seldom prevails over the primal

urges drawing lovers together. So this survey of qualifications is offered especially to married couples who want to lay the foundation
for a more satisfying and spiritually fruitful relationship.

Five

Self-Commitment

Are you willing to live consciously, claiming personal responsibility for your life?

Being a friend to yourself is no mere metaphor or purely sentimental idea. It is the basis of all relationship, because it is a fundamental recognition of soul.—Thomas Moore[1]

Marriage is our last, best chance to grow up.—Joseph Barth

Remember, we're all in this alone.—Lily Tomlin

The vocation of marriage primarily involves work on ourselves. Self-commitment is even more fundamental than the usual emphasis on commitment to a partner. Paradoxically, self-commitment enables us to better love our mates. The way we relate to ourselves determines how we relate to others.

Do you love and respect and nurture yourself? On that basis, you are equipped to love, respect and nurture your mate. If you fail to honor yourself in these ways, you cannot possibly honor your mate. Nor can you graciously receive what your mate — or God — has to offer.

Self-Knowledge

The first duty of self-commitment is to investigate the full, complicated truth about ourselves. Self-delusion and naiveté must give way to thorough discernment of our strengths and weaknesses, our hopes and fears. Because life continually changes us, this commitment to self-knowledge calls for lifelong expansion of our subjective frontiers. Only conscious individuals can approach the goal of conscious relationship.

Beyond self-examination, we gain perspective by heeding the comments of others who know us well. We can count on our mates, especially, to point out our failings. They gladly cast light on our blind spots, if we're humble enough to scrutinize our reflected image.

Self-commitment calls us to embrace the full scope of personal reality. We must acknowledge our destructive potential along with our essential goodness. By claiming even the monsters in our nightmares as our own, we honor the fullness of creation — and improve the odds of containing our inner beasts. Learn to tolerate the darkness in your own soul, and you'll be better able to love your equally complicated mate.

Self-acceptance promotes friendly curiosity about other people. You'll begin to regard their quirks not so much as irritating flaws, but intriguing mysteries. With this attitude, you and your mate can sustain fascination with each other throughout a married lifetime, paying tribute to the genius of God's creation.

Moods and needs

Self-knowledge begins with recognition of the small truths: the moods and preoccupations that establish our personal reality, and form a context for all other experience. So pay attention to spontaneous emotions, fantasies and longings.

Proper exploration of this rich, inner world does not require deep analysis. Simple curiosity and wonder are all you need. These attitudes prompt reflection on the varied forces that animate our lives. Sometimes, for example, a character in a movie, an image in a magazine, or a chance encounter with a stranger evokes a potent intrigue. Instead of dismissing such a "foolish" allure with a contrived explanation, you could honor that vague stirring by taking a minute to daydream about it.[2]

These fleeting, interior events may or may not correspond to any external reality. Granting them attention may distract from the task at hand. Still, they deserve regard, because every other perception must filter through this subjective tangle before we can apprehend it. How can you give fair consideration to a proposal from your mate, unless you notice how today's mood colors your initial reaction?

Next, self-knowledge means recognizing our own needs. Beyond the basic material requirements for survival, each of us has an array of needs (for friendship, affection, etc.) which we can satisfy only in relationship. These needs not only vary from one person to another, but fluctuate from time to time in the same individual. On one occasion, we may yearn for greater closeness with our mates. On another, we may need solitude in order to sort our thoughts and feelings. Only through refined awareness of our shifting needs can we invite our partners to care for us properly, according to our distinct requirements.

Throughout his career as a draftsman, Jack prided himself on his capacity to work independently, without any need for direction or approval. He routinely insisted that he had no needs whatsoever. And who could dispute the claim? He certainly never asked for anything.

Jack counted himself a maverick, with a temperamental preference for working alone. He had great confidence in his abilities, and little use for the opinions of others. His personal estimation of a job well done provided all the satisfaction he required.

Retirement upset this orderly picture. Suddenly cast loose from the structure and meaning he derived from his work, Jack feels utterly adrift. He's restless and often cantankerous. His wife complains that he's always underfoot, meddling in her activities, and criticizing her performance in household matters he knows nothing about.

Contrary to Jack's contention that he has no needs, he simply took the fulfillment of his minimal needs for granted. Retirement undermined this pose of self-sufficiency, advancing a crisis with spiritual implications. To resolve it, he must first recognize his reliance on work to give his life meaning. Now he will have to find an alternative justification for his existence, in order to make peace with progressive bodily decline. Eventually, he may learn the benefits of reaching out to his wife, drawing simple meaning from their shared days.

Personal history

Besides paying attention to our own moods and needs, a commitment to self-knowledge calls for an inquisitive attitude about the historical forces that shaped our personalities. The events and circumstances of childhood obviously top the list of critical influences. It doesn't require advanced training in psychology to recognize the significance of childhood poverty, chronic illness or frequent relocation.[3]

Even more important than these environmental conditions, the treatment we received from our caretakers leaves an indelible imprint. Were your parents affectionate and available, or cold and distant? Did they treat you with respect or with scorn? These formative relationships (along with the model of interaction between our parents) undeniably color our hopes, fears and capabilities for intimate relationship in adulthood. They also frame our implicit expectations of God.

Yet, in psychotherapy, I routinely encounter people who show an utter lack of curiosity about their own past, as if it were unworthy of consideration. Such an attitude often indicates a painful history they would prefer to forget. In other cases, it attests to indoctrination in the misguided belief that any self-inquiry amounts to conceit.

Many of these people count it a virtue to shun examination of childhood. They proudly rationalize it as a matter of taking responsibility for their adult lives. Personal responsibility is a worthy goal, best achieved by recognizing the factors that shaped our current reality — the better to sort out which ones we can control. Understanding the past helps us see what needs change in the present.

The same principles apply to more recent life history. We need not scrutinize every detail, in pursuit of explanations. Simple reflection helps us appreciate the wonder of human existence.

For the first five years of their marriage, Adam and Sheila occupied a tiny, rented cottage, built as maid's quarters in a former era. It served as a charming honeymoon bungalow, but after a year, they began to chafe in the confined space. They rejoiced when they could finally afford a larger place.

Today, though, as they scurry from room to room, packing up the last boxes, Adam feels strangely edgy. He promptly dismisses the mood, attributing it to the strain of all the transition arrangements. Then, he finds Sheila sitting on the floor of their empty bedroom, with tears streaming down her face.

"We don't have time for this," Adam thinks, sighing irritably. "What's the matter with you? You should be happy." Before he can speak, though, he spots the open photo album in her lap. Sensing his presence, Sheila looks up and extends her arms to him. Adam reluctantly lets her pull him down beside her.

"I know I shouldn't be taking time for this now, but as I packed this, it fell open to these snapshots from our early months here. Remember this little garden we planted that first spring together? Everything was so beautiful and we were so happy."

Adam hugs her. He feels a little self-conscious with all this nostalgia, but some of his tension begins to melt away.

Honoring the past, we facilitate the present. Recalling our history, we're more likely to build on previous triumphs and avoid previous pitfalls. As we're reminded of our own foolishness and inconsistency, we become better able to accept our partners in all of *their* eccentric ways.

Marriage seals the commitment to self-knowledge. It exposes all our rough edges, forcing us to confront ourselves starkly. Painful as this self-encounter may feel, it fosters the gradual emergence of our best, true selves.

Personal Responsibility

Above all, self-commitment means that we assume ultimate responsibility for our own welfare. At the most fundamental level, we bear a duty to honor our bodies by dedicating the necessary attention to health, safety, fitness, hygiene and grooming. Do you eat a healthy diet? Do you make time for regular exercise and adequate sleep? Do you always buckle your seat-belt in a car?

Consider also how you negotiate your higher needs for friendship, affection, sexual fulfillment, meaningful work, intellectual stimulation and recreation. In many of these domains, we cannot adequately fend for ourselves. We must reach out to others. This shows integrity, admitting our true condition as creatures of need.

Personal responsibility calls us to face every challenge life presents. It means never giving up on ourselves. Instead, we forgive our failings, resolve to correct our mistakes and adapt to our limitations. This demands humility and courage. At times, we feel depleted, overwhelmed and afraid. Still, we must forge ahead.

In all facets of self-care, we naturally follow the example of our early caretakers, treating ourselves as they did. At best, our parents supplied a model of calm, conscientious guardianship. If they performed their duties grudgingly, we're apt to regard our own needs as a burdensome inconvenience. We may also try to hide our needs, expecting an unsympathetic response.

If our parents failed to encourage our blossoming capacity to provide for ourselves, we may feel dependent and confused about our needs, even as adults. If our parents watched over us apprehensively, fearful of making a mistake, we may incline to a comparably fretful attitude, mistrusting our own judgment. Children taught to feel ashamed of their own basic requirements suffer the most grievous injury. They shy away from even admitting any needs, let alone entreating others to help satisfy them.

For some combination of these reasons, many people try to minimize their needs. They pretend self-sufficiency, and reject offers of support. Or they manipulate others to take care of them, without conceding the debt. These maneuvers amount to spiritual arrogance, a denial of humanness, and a rejection of love. Furthermore, any uneasiness about our own needs will taint our attitude toward the needs of our mates.

Most of us are drawn to marriage because we prefer collaboration over an isolated, individual stance. For some people, this desire for togetherness cloaks a dread of solitude, and a feeling of insufficiency. They implicitly hope a mate will shelter them from the trials of life. This passive-dependent expectation is not only unrealistic; it also smacks of idolatry, trying to make the relationship substitute for God. Anyone harboring such a vain hope will suffer bitter disappointment in marriage. No human relationship can furnish complete fulfillment.

Certain other people, while made of sturdier stuff than this, shirk responsibility indirectly. By focusing all their energy on supporting (or trying to reform) their mates, they neglect the duty to satisfy their own needs, pursue their own dreams, and correct their own faults. They justify their overly solicitous conduct as devoted self-sacrifice, toward the eventual goal of greater mutual exchange. They overlook a fundamental law of human relationships: You win respect by showing self-respect. Other people will treat you roughly the same way you treat yourself.

Shunning these evasions of responsibility, our focus shifts to the only person we have the power to change: ourselves. We must rely on our own resourcefulness to solve our problems. That's not to say you should blame yourself whenever you're unhappy. Self-blame actually constrains responsible behavior. It undermines confidence, stalls initiative and inhibits common sense. Responsibility is literally the ability to respond. Cultivate this ability, and you embrace married life as an adventure.

When our mates disappoint us

This personal focus is difficult to maintain, because marriage activates primal longings that hark back to childhood. Most of us enter marriage expecting empathy, acceptance, support, companionship and physical satisfaction. When, at times, we feel misunderstood, rejected, undermined, lonely, or sexually frustrated, we're apt to blame our mates for failing to deliver what they owe.

Some people think this justifies manipulation. They plead, scold, rage, wheedle and whine, in the mistaken belief that their mates possess the key to their happiness. In this futile quest, they sacrifice their legitimate power, as well as their dignity.

When our mates prove unable or unwilling to provide for our essential needs, we must shoulder the duty to make alternative provisions for ourselves. We must claim responsibility for the fulfillment of our own needs. This forces a profound shift in perspective on the inevitable conflicts of marriage.

Ordinarily, when domestic troubles arise, we implicitly ask ourselves, "Why is my partner behaving so badly? What can I do to make her change?" From a practical point of view, the answers are straightforward. My partner's "bad" behavior is triggered by her relationship with me. There's probably nothing I can do to make her change.

In presuming to know how our partners ought to change, we create a diversion from our own issues. Marital conflicts prick old wounds, and highlight personal failings that point to how we need to heal and grow. This feels threatening, so most people try to dodge such realizations. They want to remain comfortable at their current level of development. God has higher aspirations for us. So God made us in such a way that we feel drawn to intimate relationship, which in turn, confronts us with ourselves.

Recognizing the futility of trying to change our partners, we're left with questions about ourselves. What am I doing that elicits my mate's unwelcome behavior? Why is it so annoying to me? What feelings about myself does it evoke? How can I adjust my attitude so it bothers me less?

Our mates can have legitimate reasons for failing to meet our needs. First, they may not understand precisely what we want. Plain and simple as our needs appear from within, another person can easily overlook or misconstrue them. Conflicts often arise from assuming that our partner's needs resemble our own.

Today, Ron and Cheryl arrive home from work much later than usual. Ron is ravenous. So it irks him when Cheryl dawdles with the mail instead of getting ready to go out for dinner as they had planned.

When Cheryl ignores a couple of testy prompts, he suddenly erupts in a fury. He accuses her of selfish disregard. She justifies herself, explaining that the mail contains a letter from an old friend, long out of touch.

After a few minutes of nasty, unproductive argument, a crucial fact emerges: Cheryl took a late lunch. She was oblivious to Ron's keen hunger, having little appetite of her own. Once apprised of his famished state, Cheryl willingly defers to his need, saving her letter until after they place an order for food at a nearby restaurant.

On other occasions, our mates will fail to deliver in timely fashion, despite a clear awareness of our urgent need. A partner with the best intentions may still have trouble getting it right. For example, everyone knows the frustration of trying to specify exactly where and how hard to scratch an out-of-reach itch.

The same problem often arises while giving directions for sexual touch. You might expect that your mate could easily please you, with a good-faith effort. But erotic needs are idiosyncratic. They are often very subtle, or even shifty. Like a literal itch, they sometimes defy expression, especially amidst urgent desire.

The challenge to contain our own needs

We cannot always trace our disappointment to problems of communication. Commonly, the needs of husband and wife stand in outright conflict. One side may sympathize with the other's plight, but still, quite appropriately, decline to sacrifice her own needs in favor of his. Or, as in the following example, circumstances may render one party physically unable to provide what the other has good reason to expect.

Melissa dreads her arrival home from a three-day business trip. Last night, talking to her husband on the phone, she could sense he had something important on his mind. At first, Bill evaded her inquiries. When pressed, he explained that on the day of her departure, a company reorganization had been announced at his workplace. The good news: he still has a job. The bad news: his workload will double, with no salary increase.

"You know I've been unhappy in this job for years," Bill said. "Last night, sitting here alone, I got to thinking maybe this is a good time to break away and start my own company, like I always dreamed of doing. I've drafted a ten-page business plan. I can hardly wait for you to get home so we can go over it together."

He was full of ideas, brimming with enthusiasm. Despite her fears about this venture, Melissa believes in her husband. She also found his outburst of boyish excitement terrifically endearing. She hated to cut him off, but it was past midnight, and she had a grueling day ahead, before her expected arrival home at 6 p.m. They agreed that Bill would pick her up at the airport. Then they could devote the entire evening to reviewing his proposal.

Now, less than twenty-four hours later, that conversation is a hazy, distant memory. Melissa couldn't sleep well afterwards, alone in a strange bed, her mind buzzing. The next day, her meetings ran overtime. Despite a frenzied dash through rush-hour traffic, she missed her flight.

She immediately tried to call Bill, but he had already left for the airport, an hour's drive from their home. And he had apparently left his cell phone behind. After waiting three long hours, Melissa caught another flight that routed her through an out-of-the-way city. Finally, the pilot announces the approach to her hometown airport, ". . . where local time is 12:17 a.m."

Melissa doesn't know what to expect when she lands. She hopes that Bill has not been waiting, wondering for six hours. If he retrieved her second message from their answering machine, he knows her estimated arrival time. At best, though, he has endured a long, frustrating inconvenience. He will be

deeply disappointed about missing the chance to talk about
his career plans. Will he be angry at her for missing her flight?
Or worse, will he want to discuss his ideas on the long drive
home? Melissa only knows that she is close to collapse.

Here, Bill confronts a problem that arises over and over again in
every marriage: the challenge to contain our own needs. The ability
to soothe ourselves can prevent many of the ugliest quarrels, which
spring from mutual desperation. Each side becomes consumed with
his own suffering, allowing no consideration for the other. Unable
to contain their own needs, they lash out in fury.

The capacity for containment differs from the foolish, pride-
ful attitude of people who pretend they can satisfy their own
needs, or even that they have none. Frank disclosure of delicate
feelings or needs takes courage, precisely because we have no
guarantee of a supportive response. We must contend with the
risk of disappointment.

Neither Melissa nor Bill deserves reproach. As their example illuminates, the periodic requirement to contain our own needs resides
in the human condition. Disappointments more often stem from a
partner's limitations than from malicious withholding. Commonly,
though, one person appears culpable.

After two years of marriage, Jennifer apprehensively divulges
a terrible secret to her husband, Bart: she was sexually abused
by her father during childhood. Bart doesn't respond well. He
minimizes the seriousness of her account. He makes excuses
for her father. At times, he insinuates she may have imagined
or invited the abuse. He seems more angry at her than sympathetic. Jennifer finally flees the room in tears, devastated.

Actually, Bart is not the callous jerk he resembles here. He is
simply overwhelmed by information that flies in the face of so
many perceptions he had counted as certain. Confused and upset,

he responds with denial — the same defense that Jennifer had used for years.

None of this excuses his insensitivity. Jennifer has good reason to feel hurt and angry with him. She needs and deserves some support. Since her husband cannot immediately provide it, she must contain her need until she can find someone better able to help. Later, after Bart has had time to digest the news, and remedy his ignorance about abuse, he might respond more appropriately.

Alternatively, Jennifer could blame Bart and withdraw into her lonely, secret shame — a victim, once again. This would amount to a failure in her commitment to assume ultimate responsibility for ensuring that her needs are met.

Sometimes, neither a mate nor anyone else can satisfy an important need, because it derives from the universal human condition. There are certain issues which everyone, ultimately, must work out alone.

For weeks, Robert has been feeling strangely unsettled, without being able to name what's wrong. To the contrary, everything in his life seems remarkably right. At age forty-five, he has a solid, twenty-year marriage to Vivian, a woman he still adores. Their two, thriving, teenage children are a source of pride and joy. He holds a secure job, doing meaningful work. He enjoys good health. He maintains several enduring friendships.

Considering these many blessings, Robert feels ashamed of his discontent. But for all his efforts to brush aside this dark cloud, it shadows his days, and chills his nights.

Robert eventually broaches the matter with Vivian, one rainy Saturday afternoon. At first, she tries to kid him out of it, as if it were just a bad mood. When he insists that it's something more weighty, she starts to worry that he has grown tired of her. "Are you having an affair?" He gives reassurance that he has no complaint about her, and no interest in other women.

These fears laid to rest, Vivian listens as her husband explores his vague longing for greater adventure and new meaning in life. Robert even wonders aloud about God — something he hasn't seriously considered in years.

Two hours later, when they set the discussion aside to make dinner, they have resolved nothing. Yet, they feel especially close. Robert takes some comfort merely in having begun the inquiry in earnest. To their credit, they both recognize that this is Robert's problem — one that only he can resolve.

Of course, Robert's problem has monumental implications for Vivian. If he fails to make headway on it, their relationship will suffer as his tension mounts, and his enthusiasm for life wanes. Someone less able to tolerate the uncertainty might unwittingly provoke an argument, just to fasten upon something concrete and manageable. Many people forsake perfectly good marriages under similar circumstances. Robert's clear assumption of responsibility, and his determination to find a resolution, prove his self-commitment.

The Five Freedoms

We establish a foundation for self-knowledge and personal responsibility by practicing five elementary human capabilities: (1) perceiving, (2) thinking, (3) feeling, (4) wanting and (5) dreaming. The renowned family therapist Virginia Satir calls them the "Five Freedoms." Together, they comprise our God-given, basic operating system.

We are born with these faculties, in rudimentary form. Like most endowments, these require frequent practice in order to reach full potential. (If neglected, they atrophy to a level barely adequate for survival.) The unimpeded exercise of the Five Freedoms enables us to meet our own needs.

1. Perception is the most fundamental freedom. In order to function effectively, we must develop confidence in our ability to see, hear, taste, smell and feel the world around us. Perception is not passive. We must selectively focus attention and actively interpret raw data to render meaning from the swirling array of ambient sensation.

2. Once we have gathered information, we must put it together to formulate opinions, draw conclusions, hatch ideas, make decisions and devise plans. These operations make up the second freedom, thinking. Thinking lays the groundwork for concerted action aiming to achieve our goals.

3. Our well-being especially hinges on the freedom to feel. Our emotions tell us how well our needs are being met. Emotions also mobilize our bodies to respond. For example, fear arises out of a perceived threat of harm. Beyond the subjective fright and dread, fear triggers the release of adrenaline, preparing us for fight or flight. In like fashion, sadness, anger, weariness and every other emotion serve as calls to action.

4. Perceiving, thinking and feeling orient us to current reality. This sets the stage for the next freedom, desire. Desire reaches from the carnal (as in aching for sexual gratification) to the exalted (as in longing for mystical union with God). Its object can range from the material (as in coveting a new car) to the sublime (as in yearning for love). It can dwell upon self-interest (as in a quest for healing) or upon helping others (as in zeal to feed the hungry).

5. Extending desire further into the future and the ideal, we enter the realm of imagination — a world of unbounded potential for everyone who has claimed the freedom to dream. Like our more immediate desires, fantasies can

be frivolous or profound, farfetched or realistic. We can dream of winning the lottery, or of achieving world peace. A child can imagine becoming a surgeon, or I can dream of playing professional basketball, regardless of my moderate height and advancing age.

Powerfully enabling as the Five Freedoms may be, they are not foolproof. To the contrary, these faculties are plainly subject to error. All of us routinely misperceive the environment. We make errors in our thinking, as a result of haste, ignorance or faulty logic. Our feelings sometimes point us in the wrong direction. We may want things that are not good for us, or that fail to satisfy as expected. We may dream of unattainable possibilities, leading to disappointment.

Nevertheless, misperceptions, mistaken thoughts, misplaced feelings, misguided desires and misbegotten dreams spontaneously find correction, through trial and error. As long as we persist in freely practicing these faculties, we learn from our mistakes. Not many people try to walk through a glass door twice.

Even children adjust their behavior in accord with natural consequences. One who smashes his favorite toy in a fit of frustration regrets it the next day, unless a misguided parent rushes to replace it. The memory of this loss gives him pause the next time. Reality provides excellent instruction, so long as (1) we accept the inevitability of mistakes, and (2) no one interferes with the spontaneous unfolding of natural consequences.

Claiming the Five Freedoms

The best parents strive to furnish an environment where a child can safely exercise the Five Freedoms. They intervene only to prevent catastrophic outcomes. Few children grow up in such an ideal environment. Most of us were reared by parents who never came to terms with their own limitations and vulnerabilities. Not having achieved full possession of the Five Freedoms for themselves, they could hardly champion the freedoms for their children. Instead, they tried to "protect" us from mistakes they feared we couldn't handle.

Adults routinely suppress a child who tries to practice the Five Freedoms. They interfere with even the most basic freedom to perceive. Hoping to console (or hush) a child whimpering over a skinned knee, a parent may insist, "That doesn't hurt." This contradicts the valid perception of pain, instilling confusion about what is real.

As children apply their limited knowledge and reasoning power, they inevitably display some foolish thinking. Often, they meet with ridicule designed to stifle them from voicing an opinion. "OK, Smarty Pants. Since you've got everything figured out, I guess you don't need me to fix your bicycle." This undermines the child's confidence in his ability to think, forcing a conclusion that it's safer to let others do the thinking.

Of all the Five Freedoms, feelings are probably the most assailed: "Big boys aren't afraid." "Don't you ever get angry like that again." "Stop that crying or I'll give you something to really cry about." These shaming messages teach children to disregard their emotions, alienating them from a major source of personal power.

Adults commonly presume to dispute even a child's desires. "You don't want to go outside to play now. It's too cold." "It's selfish to want so many toys." As a consequence, children come to rely on external judgments of whether to squelch or indulge their impulses. They never learn to negotiate their desires with reality. So they bend to peer pressure, or fall prey to skillful manipulation from advertisers and demagogues.

Dreams are especially fragile. When children express grandiose fantasies, an adult has the power to crush their tender imaginations with a careless put-down like, "Who do you think you are, Mr. Big Shot?" Sometimes parents extinguish fantasies without even bothering to hear them: "Get your head out of the clouds and finish cleaning your room." Eventually, children learn to stifle themselves rather than risking humiliation.[4] It should come as no surprise that so many young adults, estranged from their dreams, lack enterprising spirit. Initiative springs from imagination.

Hardly anyone escapes childhood in full possession of the Five Freedoms. By the time we leave home, we have become our own slavemasters. We unconsciously adhere to the same restrictions that our parents and teachers once enforced.

We tend to select a mate who functions at a comparable level of constraint. When one partner dares to venture beyond the accustomed limits, expressing a revolutionary thought, admitting a "foolish" feeling, or entertaining a dangerous dream, the other disapprovingly draws back on the reins. This parental stance typically evokes a childish regression into whiny protest or resentful conformance.

Either maneuver evades personal responsibility. In blaming someone else for denying our freedom, we help fasten our own chains. Instead, we must actively claim our God-given rights to perceive, think, feel, desire and dream.

John and Megan are quietly contemplating a spectacular sunset together, on the last day of their vacation. "I feel sad to think about having to go home tomorrow," Megan remarks.

"Don't be ridiculous," John scolds. "We've had a great vacation, but now we should be ready to climb back in the saddle."

Only a minute before, he too had been wistfully reviewing their holiday, wishing that it didn't have to end. But then he forcibly dismissed that line of thinking, trying to gird himself for return to work. Megan interrupted him in the midst of mentally composing a to-do list. Her idle comment threatened his resolve. Unconsciously, he tried to suppress her the way he suppressed himself — just as his father had disallowed any complaining when it was time for chores.

To her credit, Megan won't have it. "You can speak for yourself. Right now, I feel sad," she declares, more forcefully this time. "I'm sure I'll be able to take care of business when the time comes."

By claiming her freedom to feel, Megan demonstrates a commitment to herself, and invites John to do the same.

Marriage presents countless openings for personal and spiritual development. In order to capitalize on them, we must be prepared to fall back on our own strength. Not only will your mate sometimes disappoint you; on some occasions, he or she will actually try to thwart your goals. This does not mean you have a bad marriage. It's merely a pointed opportunity to build integrity.

You may have to stand alone, precisely when you feel most needy of support. When your internal resources feel insufficient, seek help where you can find it: from friends and family, from experts, from books, from God. Lack of support from your mate is no excuse for failing to do what needs to be done. We can build intimate partnership, and reach for the most exalted spiritual heights, only when we're standing securely on this platform of self-commitment.

Six

Wholesome Shame

*Are you willing to admit your limitations,
your need for change, and for help?*

*All have sinned and fall short of the glory of God. [We] are justified
freely by his grace.*—Paul's Letter to the Romans 3:23–4

Shame signals an encounter with our limitations. These limitations are fundamental to the human condition. No matter how strong, everyone can be broken. No matter how attractive and fit, our bodies eventually fall into decline. No matter how self-sufficient, we still need other people. No matter how skillful or clever, we sometimes fail. Reduced to simplest terms, we will all die. None of us is God.

These indisputable facts of limitation confront us most fiercely in marriage, where we stand uniquely exposed. They evoke feelings of consolation or despair, prompting openness or estrangement, depending on whether our experience of shame is wholesome or distorted.

What Is Wholesome Shame?

Wholesome shame equips us with the revolutionary presumption that we are worthy of love, despite our limitations. To the extent we have known unconditional love and acceptance, especially during childhood, we can tolerate the exposure of our weakness and vulnerability. Our chagrin is tinged with relief, because wholesome shame gives us permission to be human.

This is not to say we are rendered immune to embarrassment and humiliation. Wholesome shame works more like an inoculation against self-hatred. It enables us to boldly reach out for love, our dignity intact, even in the midst of apparent failings.

Wholesome shame promotes authentic humility. This happens whenever we manage to laugh at our own mistakes, vanity or clumsiness, correcting an inflated self-image. On the other hand, wholesome shame removes the constraint of false modesty that would prohibit any mention of our talents, virtues and accomplishments. We learn to strike a balance between recognition that we are ordinary (like everyone else in the limited human condition) and that we are special (by virtue of our unique gifts). The cartoon character Popeye had it right: "I am what I am."

A measure of wholesome shame is crucial to marriage. Intimacy demands honest self-presentation — a willingness to progressively disclose the unvarnished reality of our inner world. Marriage invites us to reveal all of our customary hiding places.

Pat and Stacey are shopping for a new car. For the first time in their marriage, they aren't strictly limited to economy models, since they both earned job promotions last year. Stacey still favors a modest, practical car. She points out that they also need new furniture. Pat is willing to settle for a four-door sedan, to accommodate the children, but he wants the engine and stereo upgrades, plus a high-tech steering and suspension package. These options cost several thousand dollars.

Unable to agree at the dealership, they decide to think it over for a week. Pat actively campaigns for his point of view, but Stacey isn't budging. Soon, he's straining for justifications. "It's not like I'm asking for a sports car. The bigger engine and performance package are really safety factors. They'll get you out of a jam. Come on. We don't have to scrimp this time."

"I already told you I don't think we should splurge on all those bells and whistles. If you want them so much, I'll go along. But stop whining. You sound like a kid whose parents won't buy him the latest designer athletic shoes."

"That was totally different."

"*What* was different? What are you talking about?"

After a few bewildered moments, Pat realizes that Stacey has no idea she just described an actual incident from his childhood. As an eleven-year-old boy, it had seemed like *all* the popular kids were wearing the same expensive sneakers. He desperately wanted a pair of his own, but his parents ruled it out of the question. He bargained. He pleaded. When they held firm, he felt crushed — condemned to inferior social status. He sulked for days.

"...Huh? Oh, yeah." Pat's mind is racing. He's not sure he wants to divulge this story to Stacey. It was bad enough the way his sisters teased him about the shoes, making the incident a family joke. He doesn't want to give Stacey ammunition in their debate over which car to buy. Even if she concedes to his preferences, she might forever refer to this car as his status symbol. His interior Voice of Shame is shouting, "Don't be a fool! One way or another, she'll use it against you. You'll never hear the end of it."

Pat considers making up an excuse to cover his distraction. But wholesome shame prevails, and he decides to tell the full story. Although he would like to think it has no bearing on the present circumstances, he's willing to give his wife a chance to show otherwise. "You know, Stace," he begins, "you have an uncanny ability to sniff out my weak points."

Such radical self-disclosure poses undeniable risk. If we reveal our secret vulnerabilities, our partners may indeed use the information against us, to bolster their side in an argument. More often, we don't get a choice; everyone looks foolish, at times. Wholesome shame enables us to withstand this assault on our pride, having relinquished the vain hope of passing ourselves off as perfect. Personal and spiritual growth can proceed only on this basis of admitting imperfection, vulnerability and need.

What Is Distorted Shame?

Many people implicitly believe they must attain perfection in order to win love. Childhood experience taught them that weakness and limitation render a person unworthy, inviting judgment and exploitation. Instilled with this distorted sense of shame, they regard themselves as fundamentally defective. Their self-esteem falsely hinges on how well they're doing, from one moment to the next. Reminders of limitation trigger feelings of inadequacy, and fear of rejection.

This feels intolerable. So they take desperate measures to avoid facing limitation or exposing it to anyone else. They embark on a two-pronged campaign of striving and denial.

Striving

Distorted shame drives us to *prove* our worthiness. It makes us think we have to *earn* the dignity and respect that's actually our birthright. Some people try to gain approval through their achievements. They stake their self-esteem on how much money they make, how much power they wield, or how well they perform. Others measure their own worth according to beauty or intellect.

Whatever the chosen arena, these compulsive achievers grapple to outdo the competition. To the extent they win success and acclaim, they enjoy a fragile, temporary sense of entitlement. They may even appear arrogant and self-centered during these periods of inflation. Then, as soon as they suffer a setback, distorted shame rushes in to indict them as fraudulent.

Alternatively, some people try to justify themselves by scrambling for the *moral* high ground. They strain to accommodate others, even at the sacrifice of their own legitimate needs — and often their integrity, as well. They bend over backwards to prove themselves helpful, loyal, considerate, generous and cheerful.

This strategy never succeeds in winning the love they crave. To the contrary, it often makes them targets of exploitation. So they learn to subsist on occasional crumbs of approval, taking consolation (and pride) in their sense of moral superiority, as people who care.

Traditionally, our culture steered men toward proving their worth by means of compulsive achievement, while women were relegated to more self-effacing, caretaker roles. The feminist movement loosened these gender-based assignments, creating greater opportunity for women in the workplace. But little progress has been made in challenging distorted shame, the root problem for both sexes. As a result, women have gained the dubious privilege of equal expectation to prove their worth in the career arena, on top of the duty to provide nurturing at home.

Denial

Whatever the particular form of striving, it is doomed to failure, since it aims to accomplish superhuman goals.[1] Perfectionistic claims look ridiculous in the light of our everyday blunders: We spill our coffee; we stub our toes; we say things in haste that we don't really mean. Overachievers in the grip of distorted shame cannot concede to reality, though, having staked their sense of worthiness on their success. They resort to denial and deceit, in an effort to hide the ways they inevitably fall short of their ideals.

They try to cover up their faults and mistakes. They stubbornly refuse to admit when they are wrong, or apologize when they hurt someone. They reject help. They rationalize their foolishness. When criticized, they make excuses, or blame someone else. When confronted with overwhelming evidence, they fly into a rage, or get drunk, or flee the scene, or counterattack on an unrelated issue.[2] In short, they hide their true selves, in a failed effort to fend off distorted shame.

Denial blocks personal and spiritual growth, which arise from humble admission of limitation and the need to accept help. The perpetrators of denial pose a hazard to their partners' development, as well, by projecting judgments of inadequacy and unworthiness. They continually find fault and use it to justify all manner of unkind treatment. This naturally erodes the partner's self-esteem and morale.

Denial has a chilling effect on marriage. Besides provoking countless quarrels, it completely obstructs intimacy. Few events are more alienating than when someone stubbornly refuses to acknowledge the obvious truth.

Donna would be the first to admit she knows nothing about cars, but even she can tell that this one isn't running properly. She descends the three steps leading from the house to the garage, where Frank has been working for the past several hours. He's hunched over one fender, his face thrust deep under the hood, with only the bill of his reversed cap sticking up. For a minute, she waits alongside the opposite front fender, hoping Frank will notice her presence. She grimaces every time he opens the throttle, making the engine roar.

"How's it going, Honey?" she finally calls out.

No response. Donna takes a deep breath and shouts her second try for his attention. But halfway through this short sentence, the engine sputters dead. Suddenly, she's shouting into silence.

Startled, Frank lurches up, banging his head hard against the hood. "Owww," he yelps. "Damn, that hurts. What are you trying to do?"

"I'm sorry."

"So what do you want, anyway?"

"Well, you know we're supposed to meet Gene and Naomi at the movies in just a couple hours. So I was just wondering how much longer you think this is going to take."

"I wish I knew. I finished the tune-up, but now it's running worse than ever."

"Is there anything I can do?"

Frank gives her a look of disgust. "Sure. You can recheck the timing."

Donna ignores his sarcasm, and peers under the hood. "Shouldn't this little wire thingy be connected somewhere?" she asks, lifting the loose end with her pinky finger.

"Don't be touching stuff you don't know anything about," Frank says crossly, bending down again to look. "That's not a wire. It's a vacuum hose. Of course it should be connected. Now I hope I can find where you pulled it off."

"I didn't pull if off anything. It was already dangling free."

"Don't you think I would have noticed that?"

"I don't know. It wouldn't be the first time you had tunnel vision. Maybe one of your tools snagged it."

"I'm not that careless."

"Why are you being so snotty? I'm only trying to help."

Frank tries to ignore her, but she crowds in beside him under the hood. "Maybe it could fit on that little nub," she suggests, pointing.

"Yeah, I see it. I was just going to try it there." He reattaches the tiny hose. "Now why don't you get out of here before you break something else?"

"I'm waiting to see what happens when you start it up."

"All right, all right...if that's the only way to get rid of you. You're getting under my skin, you know."

Frank slides behind the wheel and turns the key. The engine starts instantly, running at a smooth purr.

"Hooray! I fixed it." Donna claps her hands with delight.

Frank turns off the engine, slams the car door, and stomps into the house.

"Hey. What's the matter with you?" Donna calls after him. "The problem's solved. You should thank me."

When Donna came on the scene, Frank was already tense and frustrated over his failure to get the car running right. She couldn't hear him over the engine noise, but he was muttering to himself, "Come on, you idiot, think! Where did you screw up? Can't you even do a simple tune-up?"

Whenever someone takes a harsh attitude toward himself, he's sure to be unreasonably hard on others, as well. So Frank was quick to blame his wife for the loose hose she discovered. Already filled with self-contempt, he couldn't bear to think that he had overlooked such an obvious problem. Then, when she was proven right, he couldn't face her — or the truth of his error.

Donna's readiness to claim full credit suggests that she also harbors some distorted shame. Otherwise, she might have been more gracious, less needy of an ego boost at her husband's expense. Let's see how this scene might have played out under conditions of wholesome shame.

"Shouldn't this little wire thingy be connected somewhere?" Donna asks.

"Hmmm. I hadn't noticed that loose vacuum hose. That could be the problem. But I'd feel so stupid, I almost hope it isn't." He shakes his head, smiling in dismay. "How could I be so blind?"

"With so many wires — and 'vacuum hoses' — running everywhere, it would be easy to overlook."

"Well, let's try to find where it belongs. I've been staring at this so long without seeing the obvious, why don't you help me?"

Sure enough, Donna is first to spot the vacant nub. Frank reattaches the vacuum hose and starts the car. When it runs smoothly, they *both* cheer.

"Thanks, Love. You saved the day," Frank says, with real appreciation, as he lowers the hood. "But there's still one thing you need to qualify as a mechanic...SOME GREASE ON YOUR FACE."

With that, he leaps at his wife, intending to smudge her face with his own. But Donna is ready. She sensed his mischievous tone, and eludes his grasp, shrieking. After two laps around the car, she lets him catch her.

Wholesome shame enables Frank to accept that he's capable of a foolish oversight, without feeling totally worthless. For her part, Donna has no need to crow about a lucky find, especially when it might make Frank feel worse. With a measure of wholesome shame in place, routine human mistakes become the occasion for sympathetic support and shared laughter.

Shame versus Guilt

Shame is often confused with guilt. In common speech, the terms are used interchangeably. The significant difference hinges on the distinction between *doing* and *being*. Guilt is properly understood as a feeling of remorse, in recognition that we have behaved badly, in violation of our own values. Wholesome shame draws a distinction between who we are, and what we have done. It enables us to acknowledge occasions of bad behavior, without feeling disqualified in our fundamental worthiness.

Are you afraid this attitude might encourage complacent misbehavior? To the contrary, with wholesome shame in place, guilt encourages responsibility. It prompts us to humbly admit our misdeeds, and repent of them: "That's not who I want to be." It gives hope that we can do better, starting with efforts to make restitution, and reconcile with whomever we hurt.

Everything looks different in the world of distorted shame, where *any* occasion of bad behavior confers disgrace. This misconception accounts for the routine blurring of terms. From within the distorted perspective, guilt and shame look identical; anyone guilty of bad behavior stands exposed as flawed and contemptible, disqualified from love. Small wonder that distorted shame generates irresponsibility. It drives people to deny their misdeeds, or make excuses. They can't accept — or even comprehend — forgiveness.

Starting with Freud, psychotherapists have traditionally emphasized the problem of guilt. The more fundamental significance of shame has been recognized only in the last decade or two:[3] Shame regulates our lives more than any other emotion.

Shame deserves the title of *master emotion*, because it defines which other emotions are legitimate to feel. Distorted shame cannot allow for the vulnerability of fear, loneliness or confusion. Ironically, shame itself is among the many so-called "weak" emotions that are shamed and disqualified in our culture. As a result, most people have little awareness of the insidious workings of distorted shame, making it all the more influential.

Childhood Origins of Distorted Shame

It's easy to see how physical or sexual abuse would leave a strong imprint of distorted shame. In the teeth of such devastating mistreatment, where physical boundaries are violated, or basic needs are neglected, children can hardly escape the inference that they lack intrinsic value. The abuser's conduct implicitly declares, "You are worth less than me. You exist to serve my needs. Because I am more powerful, I can use you however I want. Even your body is not your own."

The roots of distorted shame are often contained in far less dramatic family circumstances, where emotional and intellectual boundaries are routinely breached. This happens, for example, during the practice of "mind-reading," where someone alleges to know another person's thoughts, feelings or motives, with no need to verify. Children subjected to mind-reading gradually lose confidence in their own intuitive wisdom, passively ceding their mental power to anyone audacious enough to claim it.

Parents convey a similar, shaming message when they inflict put-downs or negative comparisons with siblings. These judgments crush a child's fragile self-image. Worse, they infiltrate the child's mind, spawning an internalized Voice of Shame.

Most of these offenses also qualify as spiritual abuse — mistreatment that hinders spiritual development. Since children are born into the world helpless, parents provide their first, formative experience of a higher power. When parents exploit their children's weakness, they pervert this sacred trust, making it difficult to ever trust God.

On the other hand, if parents furnish reliable, affectionate nurturing, children learn that they are unconditionally precious and lovable; they learn that they can safely trust a Higher Power.

Good parents go on to demonstrate awareness of their own limitations and vulnerability, modeling wholesome shame. They hold themselves accountable for their actions, modeling healthy guilt. As children outgrow the need for the comforting illusion that their parents are omnipotent, these parents steadily relinquish this inflated role. In doing so, they implicitly point the way to relationship with an authentic Higher Power on whom they, too, must rely.

The Spiritual Implications of Shame

Shame holds far-reaching spiritual significance. Wholesome shame reminds us that we need other people and we need God. Equipped with wholesome shame, we're able to claim God's grace. We can recognize our need for it, and still feel worthy of it.

Distorted shame would keep us isolated until we could somehow work our own redemption. When someone offers unconditional love, distorted shame disqualifies it. "No, this can't be true. He doesn't know the *real* me." Thus, distorted shame tends to perpetuate itself in lonely insecurity.

Everyone harbors at least some pockets of distorted shame. We may be able to admit certain of our limitations — perhaps even laugh at them — secure in the knowledge that we are nonetheless worthy of love. In other areas of conditioned sensitivity, we persist in shame-driven striving.

Throughout Carl's childhood, his father set an example of tireless labor. This capacity had enabled his family to survive very lean times during the Great Depression. He wore this "hard worker" distinction as a badge of manly pride.

Carl always felt ashamed that he couldn't live up to his father's model. He could find no relief in his father's wish for him to find a more comfortable life of mental achievement. He simply transferred the old values to a new arena, continually feeling unable to match his father's self-discipline.

No matter how much Carl might do, he could always identify time that he had wasted. If he vowed to never again indulge his lazy tendencies, he only planted more seeds of distorted shame — having repeatedly proven that he was incapable of overcoming this character flaw through willpower.

Carl would sometimes lament to his wife about the oppressive weight of his self-loathing on this account. These complaints always seemed futile, though. After all, she had never demanded that he work harder. How could she release him from the stringent demands he placed on himself?

She could only point out his accomplishments — which he'd discount as trivial — and patiently remind him of her unqualified love. This latter gesture always struck him as not only irrelevant, but somehow irritating. So, when feeling this way, he often withdrew into a crabby, self-imposed exile.

Why would someone struggling with distorted shame reject love? When Carl is caught up in self-contempt, a part of him *doesn't want* unconditional love. Outrageous as it seems, the ego wants to be loved on merit, or else not at all. Carl was lucky. Gradually, unevenly, like an eroding seawall, his shame yielded under the persistent force of unconditional love. For most of us, such an experience of grace bestowed by another *person* paves the way to deeper acceptance of God's grace.

Healing Shame within Marriage

Marriage brings distorted shame into the open, where it might encounter grace. Over the routine course of living together, we cannot conceal our faults and limitations. Where we persist in trying to do so, our partners confront the absurd pose. Every conscious encounter with distorted shame presents a chance to resolve it to wholesome shame — a chance to discover the availability of love, despite our failings.

We must already possess some measure of wholesome shame in order to jump start this healing process. How else could we muster the courage to admit our imperfection, risking rejection and humiliation? We must be able to entertain the prospect of being found worthy of love, just as we are. Even granting a favorable response (like Carl received from his wife) we may need to revisit the same tender issue many times, over a period of years, before we can truly accept ourselves as lovable in the midst of our failings.

Couples often skirt distorted shame because it always provokes a fight. This practice may begin as well-meaning consideration for the partner's sensitivities. But over the long term, avoidance breeds alienation. Resentment accumulates over the prohibition against mentioning the elephant in the parlor. This resentment periodically erupts in snide remarks.

From the day Jodie met Ben, she knew he lacked physical coordination. Anyone observing him walk down the street could see that he's a hulk of a man, with an awkward gait. It would never occur to her to hold this against him. If anything, she regarded it as part of his charm, especially in combination with his kind, gentle nature.

Not until their wedding day did Jodie discover the extent of Ben's sensitivity about his clumsiness — and how abruptly it could sour his mood. The ceremony proceeded without a hitch. Everyone attending the reception was caught up in the festive spirit. When Jodie's maid of honor whispered in her ear that it was time for the bride and groom to lead off the first dance, it so happened that Ben was not at her side. Jodie easily caught sight of him, though. As she hurried across the ballroom, she could feel everyone's eyes following her, as the band struck up the introductory bars of a waltz.

"The first dance with my handsome husband..." Jodie said, beaming with delight. She seized his hand and turned to stride out onto the dance floor. Ben remained firmly planted in place, nearly jerking her off her feet when she reached their arms' length.

"N-n-no, I don't want to," he stammered.

"Oh, don't be silly. It's a tradition. No one expects us to look like Fred Astaire and Ginger Rogers. Come on," Jodie coaxed.

"No. I don't dance," Ben insisted more firmly. True, they had never gone dancing during their courtship. Jodie wasn't especially fond of dancing either. She wouldn't have cared if they never again danced together, after today.

"Be-en. Everyone's watching and waiting for us. We have to. Please," she pleaded.

"I said, 'I don't dance!'" he snapped, raising his voice. With that, he turned and walked away, leaving her standing alone, mortified, gazing at the back of his broad, crimson neck.

Jodie turned to face a roomful of stunned stares. She managed a weak smile, made an exaggerated shrug, and fled the room. The bandleader did his best to cover her retreat, calling out, "OK. *Everybody* dance."

Later, Ben apologized profusely. "I just couldn't do it. I was paralyzed," he tried to explain. "I probably would have stepped on you, or tripped or something. I would have made a fool of myself."

"So instead, you were willing to make *me* look like a fool," Jodie shot back. "How could you do that to me?"

With neither of them able to see the other's point of view, they went on as best they could, hoping to forget this unfortunate incident. Thereafter, Jodie tried to refrain from testing his coordination, but she found it impossible to avoid piquing his shame from time to time.

Today, for example, as they are preparing dinner, she playfully tosses Ben a potato across the kitchen. He fumbles it. "I wish you wouldn't do stuff like that," he says peevishly. "You know I hate to be reminded what a klutz I am."

"Who do you think you have to impress?" Jodie demands, suddenly overcome with exasperation. "Can't you see that I love you...that I don't care if you're a big, clumsy oaf?"

She doesn't mean to insult him. She wishes she could retract the slur. Since she can't, she wishes that he would at least fight this out with her. Instead, characteristically, he slinks away. She *throws* the second potato, hitting him hard in the back.

If Ben could tolerate focusing on his shame, he might tell her about the humiliations of his childhood, including the merciless teasing he endured from other boys. Even more excruciating was his father's thinly veiled disappointment that Ben could never match the athletic prowess of his older brother. Disclosure of these painful memories would almost certainly stir Jodie's compassion. As matters stand, his sensitivity appears foolish and weak. She increasingly resents the tedious burden of trying to shield him from any encounter with his shame. Pressure on Ben will continue to mount, until he's able to risk reaching out for love, even amidst exposure of his limitations.

Resolving distorted shame poses a lifelong challenge. The task may seem overwhelming, when the problem first becomes evident. Gradually, though, the relief of shedding pretenses reinforces the process. Contending with shame becomes less like crossing a minefield, and more like an Easter Egg hunt. Each discovery of distorted shame becomes a welcome opportunity to claim greater freedom, spontaneity and love.

Shame is a pivotal issue in spirituality. More than any other factor, the caliber of shame that bride and groom bring to marriage determines their likelihood of success in creating a spiritually fruitful union. Marriage provides the ideal context for cultivating wholesome shame. Engaging this challenge will test the next qualification, your Desire to Live a Shared Life.

Seven

Desire to Live a Shared Life

*Are you willing to actively pursue deeper
knowledge of your mate, and likewise open
your heart for inspection?*

If marriage is not the prime concern of your life, you're not married.
—Joseph Campbell[1]

To sustain vitality in marriage, you must bring a strong desire to
share your life with your beloved. This desire begins with curiosity about your mate's private, inner life, along with a corresponding
readiness to open a window onto your own subjective world. These
attitudes arise spontaneously when you first fall in love, but need
reinforcement to prevail through the times when you may feel *out*
of love. You must constantly renew the commitment to maintain
your relationship as the top priority in life. In practice, this means
continual efforts to enlarge mutual understanding, and find joint
solutions to any problems.

This goes well beyond the conventional standards of marital commitment. Formal wedding vows emphasize perseverance through potential adversity ("...for better or worse, for richer or poorer, in sickness and in health") and sexual fidelity.

The statistics on divorce attest to the difficulty of honoring even these basic commitments. Yet, perhaps we expect too little, rather than too much. Any slacker can passively fulfill the pledge to refrain from adultery and abandonment, merely by planting himself on the sofa. With this limited vision, is it any wonder that so many people find marriage lifeless and confining? Should someone claim pride in honoring his marriage commitment, having done no more than endure a drab arrangement of cohabitation over the years, out of fear that no one else would find him acceptable?

The vocation of marriage calls for a more comprehensive commitment, expressed in action. In practical terms, the essential ingredients of this commitment are time and attention devoted to intimacy. Attempts to understand your mate must be balanced with active self-disclosure. Sharing your life with another person draws upon the same capacities for wonder and self-surrender that are vital to any spiritual quest.

Time and Attention

Nothing else can substitute for unstructured time together with your mate. Go for a hike, or an after-dinner stroll around the block. Watch a sunset. Attend a baseball game. Take a scenic drive, or tour a park; prepare a picnic for two. Go fishing from a small boat. Make a sand castle at the beach. Huddle around a campfire. Gaze at the stars. For an especially romantic outing, visit an art museum.

Even while staying at home, arrange to spend unstructured time together. Lounge in bed for a while after awakening on a weekend morning. Snuggle up on the sofa and listen to music. Take a bath together. Savor shared meals, without television. Other, more goal-directed activities, such as baking cookies or playing a simple board game, can serve as well, if conducted in the same leisurely spirit, without too much regard for efficiency.

These pastimes call for only intermittent focus, leaving room for spontaneous conversation. While taking a walk, for example, either party can remark on the scenery, or launch discussion of a deep yearning:

> "Lately, I've been thinking more and more about having children, even though I know we really can't afford it yet."

Or someone might follow up on a prior remark:

> "Do you remember the other day when you said you've been feeling restless lately? That stuck with me. I've been wondering what you meant."

The shared background activity maintains an ongoing link to each other, bridging any lapses in conversation. Shared silences are essential to intimacy, because they promote reverie. When dormant memories and vague ideas bubble to the surface, don't hold back, to sift them privately. Speak up right away. When your partner has something to say, listen carefully, with a curious attitude.

Some people object that this sounds too much like work. They expect marriage to provide a comfortable haven from the strains of their extramural lives. Undeniably, attentive listening requires some discipline to set aside your own agenda and focus on your mate. If he or she is upset about something, the task grows even more strenuous.

Complaints that this amounts to *too much* work indicate poorly developed skills in the art of listening. Any complex activity feels taxing until we achieve a basic level of mastery. It's like learning to read. A beginner, self-consciously straining to recognize each word, can barely follow the narrative. A proficient reader becomes absorbed in the content, unconscious of a process that once felt labored.

The same holds true for reading people. Listening gets easier as we overcome self-consciousness, and shed the misplaced duty to resolve whatever feelings or problems we hear. Gradually, we become more adept at listening between the lines.

The inclination to pay attention grows with love. Anyone who sincerely desires a shared life will find many ways to show it, regardless of conversational skill. We express interest through careful observation on one occasion, through considerate action on another, or yet again with merely a look or a touch.

Why is it so important to pay attention to our mates? Like the delicate detail of a flower, the most fascinating aspects of a person become apparent only upon close inspection. When we look closely and probe deeply, we honor each other. We implicitly affirm, "You are someone precious and valuable, worthy of careful notice." This message summons the best qualities our mates have to offer, confirming our positive expectation. The following example shows how human nature thrives in the warm light of inquisitive attention.

One lazy summer afternoon, while admiring her flower garden in the backyard, Anita feels a sudden inspiration to portray the scene in a painting, although she hasn't painted since high school art class. Her husband, Ray, embarked on a long bike ride only half an hour ago, and the kids are spending the day at an amusement park with friends, so she knows she'll have some uninterrupted time. But she resists.

"I'd probably just make a big mess." With that discouraging thought, Anita sets about plucking a few dead blooms off her begonias. But when the impulse reasserts itself, moments later, she goes in search of art supplies left over from the children's last project.

Anita giggles girlishly as she hurries across the yard to the picnic table, water sloshing from a paper cup in each hand. She carefully dips a brush tip in the water and transfers it to a hard square of bright pink paint, mixing it around to get the proper consistency. Then, holding her breath, she touches brush to paper. "Mmmmm," she murmurs with satisfaction, as the color spreads on the absorbent paper.

An hour later, after several false starts, Anita appraises the completed painting with ambivalence. She feels pleased with the range of colors she was able to mix from such a limited palette. True, her control was fitful, but the composition has merit, she finally decides. She carries the painting indoors, setting it aside to dry on the desk in the den.

Ray arrives home sooner than expected, just after Anita finishes her cleanup. He bounds into the den, wiping his face with a towel. "Hi, Love." He's drenched in sweat, so they lean over, touching only at the lips for a salty kiss.

"Have a good ride?"

"Terrific," Ray exclaims, beaming. "I'm parched, though. Any iced tea in the 'fridge?" Anita nods frantically, gently mocking his enthusiasm. He turns on his heels, heading for the kitchen, but pulls up short of the door, bending over to peer at her painting on the desk. "Whoa, what have we here?"

Anita hadn't anticipated this moment. "Oh, that's nothing," she stammers, feeling oddly flustered. "...but don't drip on it."

"Oh, yeah, right." Ray stands upright and towels his face again. "I wouldn't want to spoil it. It's beautiful. The colors are so vibrant. And I love the way this clay pot in the lower corner draws my eye across the page. Where did you get — wait a minute.... This is our yard! Who painted this?"

"Well...I did. Just now, while you were gone."

"You're kidding. Have you been taking art classes on the sly? I had no idea you could do something like this. It's very good."

"Do you really think so?"

"I'm no art critic, but I know what I like. Bring it out to the kitchen while I get something to drink."

Ray shakes his head in amazement as he pours the iced tea. "I just can't get over how I've been married to you for ten years without realizing you have this artistic talent." He gulps some tea. "Sure, I've always deferred to your taste in matching shirts and ties. But this painting looks like something you'd see hanging in one of those boutique art galleries, for several hundred dollars."

Anita laughs. "I doubt it. But tell me more."

A minute passes in silence as Ray examines the painting. "I love these rich, saturated colors," he says finally." How did you get this rosy-brownish-orange color? It captures the marbled tints of the flagstones just perfectly."

"You basically figured it out. Just one tint over another. Aren't watercolors great?"

"Gorgeous. I also like how the pots are kind of...well, lopsided—in a good way, I mean. It gives them character. What made you think to do that?"

"I can't claim it was calculated. That's what happens with watercolors when you lose control."

"Matisse would have said, 'I meant to do that.'"

"So you think it's good enough to post on the refrigerator door?"

"No way. I want to frame it," Ray insists.

Throughout the afternoon, Ray refers back to the painting again and again, as other questions and comments occur to him. This prompts Anita to tell some funny stories from her art classes which had never come up in all their years together. She recalls winning a school prize with one of her projects. "For months afterwards, I dreamed of running away to Paris, to live in a garret and set up my easel along the Seine each day."

Charmed by this romantic fantasy, Ray joins in elaborating it further. "Maybe I could sell your creations from one of those carts with big wheels. Around noon each day, when the overhead light gets too harsh for painting, we could dine on baguettes, cheese and wine. Then we could go back to our little room for a short nap and.... By the way, how long until the kids get home?"

By showing interest, we cultivate interest. This bootstrap process enables us to avert boredom over the course of a married lifetime. Only through energetic exchange of cutting-edge, personal knowledge can we maintain a vital, long-term bond.

The vignette also illustrates the interplay between attention and the other side of the transaction, self-disclosure. Ray's expression of interest encourages Anita to reveal additional, tender aspects of herself. These fresh revelations further reinforce his attention, and so on, in an ascending spiral of intimacy.

Self-Disclosure

Any subject grows dull in the absence of meaningful variation. No one spends much time watching grass grow. We are biologically geared to explore new terrain, in search of fresh opportunities. Prehistoric human survival depended upon this instinct. Our nervous system automatically orients to *changes* in our surroundings — especially changes related to safety, and feeding or mating opportunities.

The Coolidge Effect

We can easily observe the magnetic power of novelty in patterns of sexual interest. New partners and fresh circumstances stimulate intrigue, while we tend to lose interest in what has become stale through over-familiarity. This has been termed the Coolidge Effect, based on a widely reported (although unsubstantiated) story about our 30th President.

> Calvin Coolidge and his wife were taken to visit a chicken farm. Mrs. Coolidge, touring separately, was fascinated by the energetic mating behavior of a rooster that she observed atop a hen. She asked how many times the rooster could be expected to perform each day. "Dozens of times," the guide assured her. "Please tell that to the President," she said.
>
> When Mr. Coolidge later arrived at the chicken coop, the guide duly informed him of the rooster's virility. "Is it with the same hen every time?" the President asked. "Oh no. He mates with as many different females as he can find," the guide explained. "Please tell *that* to Mrs. Coolidge," said the President, triumphantly.

This anecdote attests to the extramarital attractions that afflict most people (especially men) after a few years of marriage. Our evolutionary heritage programs us to maintain mating relationships for only about four years.[2] This roughly corresponds to the length of time, under nomadic conditions, that a human newborn requires dual parenting, in order to have a reasonable chance of survival to adulthood. Natural selection favored males who sought a new mate every few years, giving them fresh opportunity to transmit genetic material into subsequent generations.

From this biological perspective, the ideal of lifelong, monogamous marriage appears distinctly unnatural. Even devoutly committed couples have extramarital longings from time to time, unless they suppress the full range of desire. Sexual fidelity — as a *spiritual* discipline, aiming for *spiritual* benefits — calls for active measures, beyond merely resisting the natural temptation to stray.

To maintain our mate's interest, we must actively open our hearts and minds for investigation, volunteering raw observations and feelings. We must risk exposing our coarse inner workings, even when they are unflattering, or even when they undermine our side of an argument. Revealing ourselves so boldly is at once frightening and exciting.

Self-disclosure nourishes both parties. First, it facilitates self-understanding. We often discover ourselves only as we attempt to formulate an expression to someone else. We also honor the recipient of the privileged information. By openly presenting ourselves, we affirm the value of our partner's response, conveying respect and trust.

Privacy and Time Apart

Everyone sets limits on self-disclosure. We feel a deep ambivalence about making ourselves transparent — even to God. On one hand, we yearn to drop all pretense, in hope of absolute empathy, acceptance and support. Much romantic longing feeds on this fantasy. On the other hand, we recoil from the prospect of divulging our shameful secrets, dreading judgment and exploitation.

A shared life does *not* oblige us to blurt out every half-formed thought or feeling that springs to mind. To do so would violate our mate's boundaries, as well as our own. Even in the closest relationship, some measure of privacy is both a right and a duty.

Each of us bears responsibility to judge what's *appropriate* for disclosure, taking into account the sensitivities on both sides. To cite an extreme example, suppose that Tom recognizes a growing attraction to a colleague at his office. Their intense collaboration on a special project sparks a gratifying sense of partnership. Tom has always been faithful to his wife, Helen. But now, for the first time, he feels conflicted.

Should Tom disclose the temptation to Helen? Perhaps not. How can he reasonably expect her to respond constructively? How can she help but feel threatened? This is *his* problem, despite the obvious implications for his wife. Only he can resolve it, by asking himself a tough question: What marital challenge is he avoiding by way of this infatuation? If he needs help making sense of what's happening, and redirecting the energy back to his marriage, he should turn to a more objective source of counsel than his wife. Commitment to honest self-disclosure does not relieve us of the duty to exercise good judgment.

Likewise, the earlier emphasis on devoting time and attention to our partners does not exclude spending time apart. Careers, hobbies, friends, extended family, and community work all deserve a place within marriage, even when they compete for limited available hours. These concerns provide a vital context for the unfolding relationship. For certain periods, they may even occupy center stage, but always against a backdrop of ongoing mutual inquiry and support. If these basic connections start to wane, priority must shift back to fortifying the relationship.

When our mates are present, we modify our behavior to accommodate them. We may unconsciously censor our speech patterns, and shy away from topics they find boring. We may forgo playing certain music, cooking certain foods, or attending certain types of movies they dislike, in order to foster solidarity and avoid giving offense. This willingness to compromise shows appropriate consideration.

Still, our legitimate, separate interests deserve expression, either alone or with like-minded friends. Neglecting to do so, we sacrifice our unique personal identity, along with some of our integrity. This diminishes not only the individual. When partners reduce themselves to their lowest common denominators, they upset the delicate chemistry of their original attraction, with all its transformative power. They trade provocative diversity for a comfortable, but stale, conformity.

Marriage should help us to manifest our true selves, distinct from all others. We are enriched not by forcing a sentimental pretense of sameness, but by the stimulating encounter of differences. Toward this end, a hearty, shared life alternates between time together and time apart.

Over the years, couples also naturally tend to assume some specialized duties. One partner may do most of the cooking, while the other maintains the yard. One writes the checks to pay bills, while the other oversees household repairs. This division of labor promotes efficiency and healthy interdependence.

But it can easily lapse into a childish dependency, eroding basic life skills on both sides. While counseling individuals who lost a mate through death or divorce, I have encountered men who are incapable of cooking dinner or buying a pair of pants for themselves, as well as women who are terrified of seeking a simple car repair. The ideal of *one flesh* never justifies forfeit of our capacity for independent functioning.

In addition to preserving separate interests and abilities, each of us must claim some time alone for quiet reflection. Everyone needs regular periods of solitude to assess personal priorities and to heed the promptings of God.

Contract or Covenant?

Marriage highlights the intrinsic tension between the desire for togetherness and the equally legitimate desire for individual liberty. Society tries to regulate these (presumably competing) interests by casting marriage in terms of a legal contract. We can better advance *both* values by understanding marriage as a covenant of love.

Contracts are essential in the business world. They list reciprocal obligations and incentives, specifying remedies in the event that one party fails to live up to the agreement. This allows the participants to collaborate, even in the absence of trust.

But a contract actually confines intimate relationship. The bid to anticipate every contingency restricts unforeseen possibilities.

The emphasis on minimum requirements constrains generosity. The stipulation of legal remedies curtails forgiveness. Contracts are inflexible. They invite a search for loopholes.

The religious concept of *covenant* provides a more suitable model for the spiritual vocation of marriage.[3] God made the prototypical covenant with the Israelites at Mt. Sinai: "I will be your God and you shall be my people"[4] God maintained an unswerving commitment to the bond, despite Israel's periodic unfaithfulness.

A covenant establishes an artificial blood kinship, signifying affection and loyalty in a climate of friendship. Although broad expectations of rights and duties are outlined for both parties, love and forgiveness take precedence over legal requirements. This allows for trust to grow, as the collaboration expands into all spheres of life.

The following example shows how a contractual mindset hinders shared life, with little compensatory gain in personal freedom.

Sally has insisted on some marital counseling, over Ralph's objection that it amounts to a foolish waste of money. Today, they arrive at my office for their first session, after two last-minute cancellations when Ralph couldn't get away from the office in time to make a six o'clock appointment.

Ralph seizes the initiative. In a booming voice, he tells me they have been married twelve years. They have three children, ages ten, seven and five. They are financially comfortable on the strength of his salary as vice-president of a large corporation. Ralph takes pride in earning enough that Sally can stay at home. He opposes her desire to seek a part-time job as soon as their youngest child starts school. He also resents Sally's "excessive" demands on his time. Finally, he nods to her, as if to give permission for her to speak.

Sally draws a deep breath, visibly marshaling her courage. "I feel like I hardly know you anymore, Ralph. And

I'm certain that you don't know me. After so many years at home, I barely know myself. We seldom talk, except about practical matters. By the time I've cleaned up after dinner, you're falling asleep. I wish we could have more of a life together, but if not, I at least want —"

Ralph interrupts, impatiently turning to address me. "I think of my marriage as a refuge from the outside world. I spend all day at the office solving problems for other people. Sometimes I don't like it, but at least I get paid. When I come home at night, I want to have a nice dinner, put my feet up and relax — maybe watch a little TV to distract myself. Is that so bad?

"On the weekends, there are always some chores to do. And Joey's Little League games. I even go to church with the family on holidays, just to please my wife. In the little time remaining, I want to enjoy myself. Maybe play a round of golf with my buddies. I do my job at the office, and Sally ought to do her job at home. Beyond that, I don't interfere with how she spends her time, and I don't want her intruding on mine."

"What *do* you want from your wife?" I inquire.

"Nothing!" Ralph shoots back. During the pithy silence that follows, he apparently realizes how stark and cold this sounds.

"I meant that I don't need anything *more* from her, beyond what she's already doing," he continues. "We have a very congenial arrangement. Or at least we did, until she got this crazy idea that we should talk more."

"But Ralph, aren't you ever curious about what makes her tick? Don't you sometimes wonder what keeps her going when she gets discouraged, what delights her, what thrills her?"

Ralph gives a look of cranky incomprehension. "I don't have time for that. Even if I did, I'd respect her privacy."

Ralph implicitly regards his marriage as a *contract* for the exchange of goods and services. By his account, he performs well beyond the provisions of that contract: He works hard to provide for all the material needs of his family; he schedules some time for family activities; he refrains from obviously bad behavior like heavy drinking or womanizing. So it offends him as unreasonable of Sally to make further "demands." Having fulfilled his duty, he expects her to leave him alone.

What's missing from Ralph's vision of marriage? He shows no interest in living a shared life. He actively resists disclosing himself. He may announce his agenda for the day, but he never reveals his dreams. He rebuffs any query of his inner world as an unwarranted intrusion.

Likewise, Ralph takes no personal interest in Sally. He neglects to inquire about her activities or her feelings. When she tries to disclose herself to him, he responds with a grunt, or ignores her entirely. This undermines her self-image as a woman with valuable qualities to offer.

Nor does he give much indication of physical desire for her. On the infrequent occasions when he initiates sex, he ventures little personal involvement. Even if Sally declines his advance (as more and more often she chooses to do) he acts indifferent. Ralph's pretense of self-sufficiency is maddening and demoralizing for her.

Breaking the Stalemate

Ralph seems unlikely to budge from his isolated stance, and Sally must set aside her campaign to change him. By clinging to a wish beyond her control, she relinquishes the considerable power she actually possesses. Does this mean abandoning her own desire for a shared life? No. It simply means doing what she can in the absence of Ralph's collaboration.

Sally could leave him, of course. But after twelve years and three children together, she prefers to exhaust every option before giving up on her marriage. Turning away from the unproductive focus on Ralph, Sally is free to define her own priorities. She cannot make him want her, but she doesn't need his consent to take a job, or do whatever else she chooses. To free some time, she might have to withdraw some of the support services to which Ralph has become accustomed.

By reclaiming the power to set her own course, Sally exerts legitimate leverage. She upsets the system that bolsters Ralph's intransigent position, forcing him to make adjustments of some kind. Perhaps these adjustments will reopen the door to a shared life. Then again, they may not. The changes that Sally undertakes for herself will work to her advantage regardless of Ralph's response. This sort of exercise in self-direction can revitalize anyone who feels stuck in a one-way relationship.

Childhood Origins of Emotional Guardedness

What can account for the emotional guardedness displayed by Ralph and so many other men? Such thoroughgoing resistance to self-disclosure usually represents a fear of exposing vulnerability. It originates in the events of childhood.

Ralph cultivated his characteristic guardedness as a way of coping with disappointments. Childhood experience taught him that appeals for help generally go unheeded. Exposing his needs brought only humiliation. So he adopted a strategy of extreme self-reliance, enduring deprivation if necessary, but asking no favors, except when he could call in a debt. Of course, he denies harboring mistrust. That would imply vulnerability. He prefers to describe himself as "independent," or "self-sufficient," or "very private."

Beyond provoking aloofness in personal relationships, childhood neglect hinders subsequent approach to God. This withholding of basic trust, so detrimental to both marriage and spirituality, can result from several different childhood scenarios.

Deprivation of mirroring

The first is simple parental neglect of the child's vital need for someone to mirror his concerns.[5] Parents who are preoccupied with their own affairs often fail to show interest in the child's perceptions, thoughts and feelings. They may even mock his childish observations.

This deals the child a stinging blow, making him feel unworthy of attention. At best, some other significant adult such as a grandparent, teacher, aunt or uncle steps forward with a show of interest. This may compensate for the parental deficiency.

Otherwise, boys are apt to internalize parental contempt for their subjective life. They shift their identification to the outer world of accomplishment. They banish any line of thought that could subvert effective action, leaving no room for fear or self-doubt. The spiritually significant capacities for awe and sympathy also wither.

Little by little, instrumental thinking becomes an unconscious mental habit. By adulthood, the young man starts to believe, "I am what I accomplish." His mind narrows to admit only practical concerns. His feelings are limited to anger (in response to anything that thwarts his intent) and satisfaction (when he steadily advances toward his goals). An actual accomplishment may feel oddly hollow; the luxury of celebration could distract from the next goal.

These men cling tenaciously to their impoverished self-concept, staunchly denying any suggestion they might be more complicated. Emotional guardedness becomes a way of life. American culture upholds this repressive strategy, which boosts productivity. It is perhaps the predominant mode of masculine consciousness.[6]

Boundary violations

If this rigid profile can result from simple neglect or shaming of a boy's subjective inner life, imagine the consequence of physical or sexual abuse. These bodily violations spur him to shield all vulnerability. He strives to preserve his integrity by maintaining an appearance of steely strength and self-sufficiency.

Transgression of *emotional* boundaries can also breed mistrust. This happens, for example, when parents insist on knowing every detail of the child's activities and inner life. Such prying violates the privacy needed to articulate a full, rich, personal identity. Parents commit an even worse breach by burdening a child with intimate knowledge properly reserved for the spouse, especially regarding the parents' sex life.

Sometimes, a boy gets cast in the role of Mommy's Prince. She grants him privileged access to herself, indulging and confiding in him, in what amounts to emotional incest. The mother inevitably exploits her power advantage to enforce expectations of how her young Prince should behave. An only child of alienated parents is most liable to this arrangement, especially if the father is physically absent.

The role of Mommy's Prince ostensibly promotes the boy to adult status, making it extremely seductive. The special, but counterfeit, closeness with his mother comes at the expense of other relationships — current and future. His father, if present, naturally resents the intrusion into his rightful domain. Guilt and fear of retaliation generalize to other male authorities, persisting into adulthood. Peer friendships also suffer. They appear drab and foolish, compared to the highly charged maternal bond.

Above all, the role of Mommy's Prince poisons future erotic relationships. Because the boy is developmentally incapable of actually fulfilling his mother's emotional needs, he carries vague feelings of inadequacy into subsequent involvements with women. He doesn't realize until much later how much of his integrity he has unwittingly sacrificed at his mother's altar.

By the time he reaches his teen years, he knows that he has been duped. Angry and confused, he resolves to prevent further encroachment on his autonomy. So he stays aloof from emotional intimacy.

Some men exact revenge through a serial pattern of manipulating, exploiting and betraying women.

The hazards of establishing masculine gender identity

Only a minority of boys suffer the abuse described above. Still, *most* men squirm at the prospect of deep, exclusive intimacy with one woman. This holds true even for men who grew up in the most healthy environments. Compared to women, we *men feel a more extreme ambivalence about close relationships*. The difference hinges on the greater hardship facing boys, when it comes time to separate from mother.

All of us, male and female alike, start life in our *mother's* womb, in a blissful state of symbiotic union with her. At birth, we suffer a rude shock of forcible expulsion into a separate existence. Thus begins the universal, lifelong conflict between striving for autonomy and longing to restore unity.

Consolidation of a separate identity poses a dual challenge. To establish ourselves as a separate person, we must set *ego boundaries*. Then we must also crystallize a *gender identity*, declaring as either male or female.

To accomplish this, a boy must make a more radical break from his mother. He proclaims to her, in effect, "I am not only separate from you; I am fundamentally different from you." He fortifies this imperative by erecting sharp, clear boundaries. He renounces not only his dependent connection to Mother, but also her feminine qualities of sensuality, gentleness, receptivity and intuition. His fledgling masculinity can afford no ambiguity. Society reinforces this stand by mercilessly punishing "sissies."

Girls are spared the trauma of such a revolutionary breach with Mother. They must still separate, of course, but gender identity presents relatively little problem. They need look no farther than their mothers for a model, identifying with the person to whom they are already bonded. Abundant cultural evidence attests to the greater gender security of women. They can dance with each other, express physical affection between themselves, wear men's clothing, and act like tomboys without any threat to their gender identity, or any cultural sanction.

The Battle of the Sexes originates in these developmental differences. Because females defined themselves by affirming the original connection with Mother, they hunger for intimacy.[7] Because we males defined ourselves by renouncing the union with Mother, intimacy threatens our hard-won masculine identity. Nevertheless, having sacrificed so much of ourselves, we ache for reunion, perhaps even more than women.

Men who feel insecure about their masculinity sometimes channel all this longing into one of its components: *sexual* desire. This limited aspect of coupling feels more manageable. A man can further dilute the risk of dependency by pursuing sexual involvement with as many women as possible. By making them interchangeable, he limits his vulnerability to any particular one.

The most guarded men show little patience for kissing and caressing, which appeal to a more playful sensibility. These activities promote awareness of the whole person, subverting his need to objectify a woman as the sum of her attractive parts. Intercourse feels safer to a man who dreads intimacy. With a narrow focus (the genitals) and a clear goal (orgasm), he's less apt to lose himself. Also, intercourse highlights the literal penetration of the *woman's* boundaries, instead of his own.

A Window of Opportunity

Falling in love presents a window of opportunity for change. A man can hardly deny his neediness when he feels so irresistibly drawn to a woman. The erotic impulse urges him to relax his rigid boundaries.[8] This stirs anxiety in a man accustomed to feeling secure in his isolation.

Sooner or later, even for Casanovas and cowboys, the longing for union surpasses the fear of exploitation. On one side of the scale, reality presses home the emotional cost of isolation. This can occur abruptly, when a man suffers a crushing setback, or incrementally, as he anticipates loneliness in middle age. On the other side of the scale, reassuring familiarity with a particular woman may lighten the perceived threat. The balance tips, and he risks exposing vulnerability.

Perhaps he accepts comfort after a loss. Perhaps he admits how much he longs to be held. Instead of humiliation, he meets with tender reassurance and heightened respect.

Such an unexpectedly gratifying experience of surrender can trigger a personal revolution resembling religious conversion. In either case, the pivotal event unleashes a rush of joy, relief and gratitude. This unaccustomed release of emotional tension validates the event. Afterwards, he feels redeemed and transformed — as if he were reborn — with new meaning in life. He regards the world in a new light, forcing reconsideration of his priorities and values. "I was blind, but now I see." An afterglow of jubilant optimism animates him for weeks afterwards.

As with sudden religious conversion, disillusionment sometimes follows. No self-respecting woman will cater to a man's insecurities forever. Even if she were to try, some sensitivity of her own would eventually conflict with coddling him. But perhaps by then, he will have become attached to this woman and the satisfactions of relationship. Perhaps he will have discovered how to love her. Having gathered sufficient desire to live a shared life, he may choose to endure the vulnerability that comes with it, opening the way to deeper relationship with his wife — and with God.

To sustain a spiritual vocation of marriage, you need a strong desire to live a shared life. This means devoting time and attention to pursue deeper understanding of your mate, even when you don't necessarily like what you find. Likewise, you must constantly push the frontier of self-revelation, even when your mate might disapprove of what you disclose. Emotional guardedness limits our acquaintance with God as much as with a human partner.

Couples joined in the Sacred Dance must also seek joint solutions to problems, forging a covenant of love that transcends practical, contractual arrangements. This draws on the next qualification, Tolerance for Conflict.

Eight

Tolerance for Conflict
Are you willing to bear the strain
of working to resolve your differences?

The fondest of couples may disagree on nearly everything.—Judith
Martin (Miss Manners)

Never go to bed mad. Stay up and fight.—Phyllis Diller

Most of us hate conflict. We especially crave peace in marriage.
Still, inescapably, conflicts arise in any vital, intimate relationship. This is not to say that ugly hostilities necessarily break out. It only means that disagreements surface, opinions clash, and feelings get hurt. At times, the needs of one person impinge on the rights of the other. None of this should cause alarm. To the contrary, conflicts present exceptional opportunities if you can withstand the heat.

The Hidden Opportunities in Conflict

Conflicts force us to reckon with the whole person, including the parts we find difficult to love. Conflicts also expose the wounds that we carry from childhood, raising prospects for healing. Finally, conflicts mark the limits of marital fulfillment, reminding us that we still need God.

Recognizing the whole person

Conflicts help us differentiate ourselves from our partners, illuminating the rich nuances of character in both parties. How else but through this awareness of complexity can we truly love a whole person? Conflicts mark the boundaries between us which only love can bridge.

Why is it so important to recognize our essential difference from our mates? Because until we do, we are essentially indulging in a private romance with ourselves. We fill the gaps in our knowledge of our mates by projecting what we want them to be. This counterfeit love diverts our attention from the unattractive aspects — which we implicitly reject — in our mates *and in ourselves*.

The characteristics that we most readily "love" in another person are of two kinds. On one hand, we love the features that are similar to what we approve in ourselves. Like Narcissus, we see our own, filtered reflection and find it quite enchanting. This happens especially during the early stage of infatuation, when fantasies of ultimate union abound.

Actual similarities (in family background, taste, values, ambitions, etc.) form a natural basis for mutual attraction. Congruence promotes compatibility. Two people holding so many features in common find it much easier to get along. They will more likely agree on considerations large and small, ranging from how to spend a financial windfall, to what they might eat for dinner.

Conflicts remind us of the substantial differences that remain, no matter how well matched. These differences force us to recognize that our mates embody impenetrable mysteries. Beginning with this one very familiar person, we become better able to marvel at every aspect of God's creation, in all of its inexhaustible (sometimes maddening) diversity. We learn to love the whole being, rather than merely what is useful or similar to ourselves. This eventually brings us back around to the challenge of regarding ourselves in the same, respectful light — not as objects to manipulate or problems to fix, but as mysteries to savor.

On the other hand, we also find it easy to "love" someone else for the qualities we lack, according to the principle of projective identification (explained in Chapter One). Mutual attractions based on projective identification are inescapable, but potentially constructive, if we strive to adopt the features that prompted our admiration. Typically, though, the charm wears thin before anyone heeds the call for personal change.

So we try to reform each other to better resemble ourselves. No one ever succeeds in this ambition, but we have much to gain from the ensuing conflict. If we shrink from it, judgmental attitudes privately solidify, blocking further investigation that could lead to deeper understanding. These private judgments reinforce an unduly favorable self-image, along with the negative perception of our mates.

By engaging the conflict, we encounter prospects for growth. We discover how to respect each other's strength, incorporating what we can, without minimizing our own strength. Likewise, we learn to accept the weaknesses and limitations on both sides.

Exposing childhood wounds

Even more importantly, conflicts are often a blessing because they illuminate the hurts from childhood that haunt our adult lives. Anyone brave enough to confront these childhood wounds has the chance to heal them, or at least receive comfort for them. We should especially stay alert for evidence of distorted shame.

Paul devotes most of his free time to woodworking. He spends countless hours sawing, sanding, routing and gluing. Everyone agrees that he makes beautiful furniture. But his wife, Denise, can only wonder at his claim to *enjoy* the hobby, since she routinely overhears him swearing and muttering while he works. He often nurses a foul mood for hours after a session in his workshop.

One Saturday, his fuming reaches such a crescendo that she fears the neighbors will think they are having a terrible fight. So she creeps into the garage to investigate. Paul rages on for a couple minutes, alternately cursing his tools and himself, before he looks up to notice her presence.

"What do you want?" he snarls.

"I was wondering what's the matter."

Paul sighs irritably. "I just get frustrated when things don't work out right."

"Why don't you set it aside for awhile if it's making you so upset?"

Paul's nostrils flare. "Why don't you go back to whatever you were doing, and leave me alone?" he counters.

No one could blame Denise for retreating at this point, but she stands her ground, despite some apprehension. "It frightens me when you get like this."

"Like what?"

"Are you kidding? For the last half hour you've been yelling and cursing like a madman."

"That's just great," Paul says, sarcastically. "First I'm stupid. Now I'm a madman."

"Who said you were stupid? Not me."

Paul's face clouds over with confusion, as he realizes she is right. "Well, I guess I must have been calling myself stupid," he concedes. "Believe me, I have cause."

"What do you mean?"

"If you must know, I mismeasured a very expensive piece of hardwood, and cut it too short," he admits, shaking his head in disgust.

"Is that so terrible?"

Paul glares at her in disbelief. "Yes! It's pretty damn bad," he roars. "For starters, it could take hours to redesign the front panel. I'll have to figure out a new scroll pattern, because the one I planned to use won't fit on..."

"Don't yell at me. I'm just trying to help."

"Well you're not helping. You're butting into something you don't know anything about."

"So explain it to me."

"What's the use? I'll only get more upset going over it again. And I can't just walk away from something like this. I won't be able to get it off my mind until I've taken care of it. Like Dad used to say, 'You screwed it up. You fix it.'"

Spoken aloud, the harshness of this mandate stuns them both into silence. Finally, Denise asks, "Did he really say that?"

Paul nods. "I remember it clearly."

"That's cold."

"Yeah, I guess it is," he says softly. "I never really thought about it before. At the time — I was maybe fourteen, and it was my first big woodworking project — it seemed reasonable enough. No different from the basic rule that all kids need to learn: 'If you make a mess, you clean it up.'"

"Sure, that applies to spilled milk and scattered crayons. Even a child can clean them up in a minute. But these are different proportions. As a kid, struggling with a man-sized job, you could have used some encouragement, and some help putting the mistake in perspective."

"Hmmm. Maybe you're right. I know I felt rotten about it, like I was a hopeless failure. I thought he meant I shouldn't show my face until I had redeemed myself. He probably didn't mean that, but that's how I took it. When Mom called me for dinner, I said I wasn't hungry. I worked straight through until ten o'clock that night before I was satisfied that I'd fixed my blunder."

"*I* want to see you at dinner tonight, no matter what."

"OK." Paul accepts her hug. "I'll try to lighten up on myself
 a little."

By standing up to conflict, Denise helps Paul recognize the source
of his unforgiving attitude about mistakes. The superficial conflict
instantly evaporates, and healing commences on the deeper issue,
once the shaming precedent comes to light.

Reminding us we need God

Ultimately, conflicts remind us that no human relationship can
provide complete fulfillment. Our mates disappoint us at times,
even in the most satisfying marriages. They often fail to understand
us. Occasionally, they're unavailable when we need them most.
Sometimes, our needs exceed their capacity to respond. At other
times, they appear to stubbornly withhold what we crave. Now
and then, their own compelling needs and insecurities may drive
them to misuse us.

To fend off discouragement, many people try to deny these in-
herent limitations of marriage. They cling to the romantic illusion
that we *can* attain perfect fulfillment with our mates — if only we
(especially the other person) could just get it right. This ideal generates hope, but it ultimately disappoints, at great cost.

Those who refuse to concede the limitations of marriage usually assess blame to account for their failed ambition. They judge
themselves — or their mates — inadequate. Some resort to serial
monogamy: "He *should* be able to gratify all my needs. Since that's
not happening, he must be unwilling or defective. I'll find someone
else who can satisfy me completely."

Others forbear from blame, but claim justification to indulge in
extramarital affairs. "Through no fault of her own, she just can't

fulfill all my needs. No one could. So I need a little romance on the side, to fill the gaps." This rationalization dilutes emotional investment in the marriage, and blunts its spiritual power.

The ultimate insufficiency of marriage in no way dims its splendor. No one faults the orchid for its faint scent. We relish its delicate beauty, without judging it deficient in any way. The limitations of human relationship simply remind us that we still need God.

The Stresses of Conflict

To capitalize on the opportunities of conflict, we must be able to withstand the attendant stresses. Aversion to conflict is often specific to family relationships. The same individuals who shun any strife at home may willingly engage conflict at work and in other business dealings, with only mild discomfort. Where love is at stake, though, the risk may appear insurmountable.

Marital conflict generates a disturbing ambivalence. We must endure the juxtaposition of anger and love, or anger and fear of losing love. One feeling frequently overpowers the other.

First, conflict threatens the love we feel for our partners. So it's tempting to excuse bad behavior, to avoid feeling angry. (Anyone who believes that anger is sinful will be especially prone to this.) Sooner or later, though, something will bother you enough that you feel compelled to action, still trying to assume the best. "He'd want me to mention this, so that he can correct it."

Hostile feelings rise up again if you receive an unsympathetic reply: "Don't bother me now." Or, "You shouldn't feel that way." Or, "I have good reasons for what I did." Defensive responses like these highlight a painful contradiction: "I love him," versus "He doesn't seem to care that he hurt me." Many people find the discrepancy so unsettling that they disregard one side or the other. Losing sight of the love, they attack. Or, squelching the anger, they withdraw.

Conflict also threatens our *supply* of love. Most of us can recall occasions of heightened vulnerability when we felt unwilling to risk estrangement from this source.

While Lloyd's wife was nursing him through a long illness, he noticed himself being extra careful not to cross her. This came partly from gratitude. Janet's tender kindness far outweighed any ground for complaint. But vulnerability gave him a second motivation to avoid conflict. Because of his physical dependency during the illness, he was afraid to jeopardize her goodwill. When trust and honesty finally prevailed, it came as a great relief for both of them to admit their fears and the weight of their burdens.

In cases of serious, chronic illness, love is often the first casualty. The patient feels afraid to risk alienating the source of essential care. The caretaker suppresses any complaints, feeling ashamed to appear selfish, when the patient's suffering seems to deserve continual priority. Such heroic aspirations deplete love.

Even in ordinary circumstances, specific fears or vague anxieties may constrain us from engaging necessary conflict. By indulging the fear, we paradoxically create the outcome we most dread. Unresolved issues simply ferment in the darkness. The suppressed anger eventually bursts out in a raging torrent, or leaks out in petty bickering, or erodes the relationship from within, leaving cold indifference.

The Price of Evading Conflict

The stereotype of marital counseling conjures a scene of unrestrained conflict, with tempers flaring and voices blaring. But many couples in therapy are actually "conflict-avoidant." They seek professional help because they have drifted apart. Some complain of loneliness, or dwindling sexual interest. Among older couples, one party may simply find no reason to persevere in the marriage, aside from regret that a divorce would upset their grown children, or shock their friends.

Marcia is a handsome, cultured woman in her fifties. Two days ago, she quietly announced to her husband of thirty years that she has filed for divorce. Alarmed and bewildered by this bombshell, Peter pleaded with her to see a counselor together. He hopes that counseling will "bring her to her senses," and save what he considers a perfectly good marriage.

Marcia conveys an attitude of steely determination, coupled with cool resignation about ending her marriage. "We lead separate lives. I decided I might just as well live alone," she explains to me, without apparent rancor. Although Peter sits nearby, she speaks to me as if he weren't present. She has evidently given up trying to explain herself to him.

"When did you first recognize this distance from your husband as a problem?" I ask Marcia.

"Oh, it's been like this for a long, long time," she responds with a sigh.

"How have you tried to correct the situation?"

"I think Peter knows I've been unhappy."

"Perhaps. But what did you do or say to call it to his attention?"

"From the beginning, I dropped hints, but he never picked up on them. Finally, a few years ago, I worked up my courage to tell him directly that I was lonely. I explained that I needed him to show more interest in me. He said he understood. He was nice enough about it at the time, but nothing changed."

"What did you do next?"

"What *could* I do? I'm not the sort of person to nag. If he wanted to be closer, he would have paid attention to what I was saying."

"Weren't you angry?"

"No. I was disappointed and hurt, of course. Humiliated, I suppose. But not really angry. Still, for me, that was the beginning of the end. Since Peter didn't seem to want me, I began to withdraw from him, too. For the last couple years, I was only marking time until the children were out of the house. I doubt if he even noticed. If he did, he never said anything."

It would be easy to fault Peter for his apparent indifference to his wife. Although he doesn't recall the critical incident, he admits that he probably dismissed Marcia's complaint as a passing mood, taking her subsequent silence as confirmation he was right. He insists that he *did* eventually notice her withdrawal, but never linked it to the earlier expression of discontent. After private deliberation, he resolved to be patient and "give her some time." He didn't know how to express his own vague dissatisfaction, anyway. "I didn't want to make a fuss."

More than insensitivity or bad faith, Peter's offense was tacit collusion in evading conflict at any price. Where only one partner holds such an aversion, the other usually succeeds in provoking an outright quarrel. In order to ignore the palpable tension of unspoken conflict, marriage partners must share a deep determination to avoid turmoil.

Couples like this do not ordinarily think of themselves as *afraid* of discord, but rather as "nice" people who simply prefer to sidestep unpleasantness. Like Peter, they count it as good manners to remain quiet rather than dispute a complaint. Like Marcia, they shrink from making personal requests without strong justification. They wouldn't want to impose "unreasonable demands." Predictably, their basic needs often go unmet. Rather than risk conflict, they unwittingly let their marriage languish.

Other people are trained to stifle grievances by a partner who interprets even a minor complaint as a global condemnation, becoming deeply hurt and demoralized: "You don't love me. I try so hard to please you, but I'm a failure." This response, arising from distorted shame, is very disarming. It effectively displaces the original complaint, demanding reassurance that everything is OK, after all. By the time the insecurity is soothed, any appetite for conflict is spent. And the threshold rises for voicing complaint. The vitality of this marriage will ebb away, until the underlying distorted shame is challenged, and the right to express dissatisfaction is reclaimed.

Origins of Conflict-Avoidance

How do some people become so sensitized to conflict, while others are willing to disturb the peace in pursuit of their legitimate needs? Genetic differences in temperament account for some of the variance. Even more, conflict-avoidance harks back to lessons drawn from how our parents handled disagreements.

Genetic temperament

Research with newborn infants shows wide variation in tolerance for intense stimulation. Most babies cry in response to sudden loud noises, looming objects in their field of vision, or jarring of their cribs. But a few seem to welcome the excitement. They smile and reach out with apparent curiosity. This early behavior represents a persistent, lifelong trait of "stimulation-seeking."

Children high in this trait are generally more active. They favor rough-and-tumble play, ignoring minor scrapes. They also fight and get into trouble more often. As adults, they like to drive fast. They prefer exhilarating sports like skiing. They are also more daring socially, and more willing to take financial risks.

These qualities may seem quite appealing, but the drawbacks are substantial. Reckless pursuit of stimulation often overrides good judgment, leading to accidents. In marriage, stimulation-seekers may provoke an argument just for sport, then walk away before it's resolved. Restless craving for the next thrill also makes them prone to sexual infidelity. Their impulsivity generates excitement at the price of chaos.

People who are very low in this trait appear timid. Reading a book or taking a walk provides ample stimulation. They are cautious, stable and well behaved, even to the point of dullness. They just don't like to get stirred up, physically or emotionally. Arguments are distasteful to them, especially at higher volumes. Still, if an issue seems important, they endure the discomfort in hope of preventing future disturbance.

So a scant measure of stimulation-seeking, considered alone, cannot explain why some couples avoid marital conflict, even at such great cost. No personality trait can account for people who tolerate conflict with anyone *except* family members. This pattern must arise from personal experience. As with other attitudes that seem to defy logic, domestic conflict-avoidance is learned at an early age, in the home.

Dire conflict in the family of origin

Either a contentious or a placid home environment can sensitize children to conflict. In a family where conflict routinely lapses into destructive fighting, the children naturally conclude that conflict is dangerous. But this lesson can generate vastly divergent coping strategies.

Scott is the older of two sons born to alcoholic parents. Looking back on his childhood, he can't recall a single day of peace in the household. Hostilities could erupt at any moment. Arguments sometimes turned violent, especially when his parents had been drinking.

Yet, Scott remained fascinated with his parents' stormy clashes. His younger brother, Jerry, would run to hide in his bedroom as soon as the yelling began. Not Scott. Of course, he wished his parents wouldn't fight. But since they did, he preferred to stick around and see what happened.

In high school, Scott ran with a fast crowd. Excitement seemed to follow him, and so did the girls. None ever stuck around for long, though. Scott had no patience for trying to resolve quarrels.

Jerry always knew that he was nothing like his brother Scott. In high school, Jerry was painfully shy. While Scott was hanging out with his friends, Jerry was at the library, studying. He envied Scott's easy way with girls, but secretly felt superior.

Scott bounced from job to job during his twenties. Then, he found success in sales, where his aggressiveness served him well. At age thirty-six, he decided it was time to settle down. He soon paired up with Rebecca, a beautiful woman, twelve years younger. Whenever they had the slightest disagreement, he quickly gave in to her wishes.

But after a few months of marriage, Rebecca realized that Scott wasn't actually conceding to her, at all. He would say anything to end the quarrel, but then do whatever he wanted, out of her view. When confronted on this, he *would* fight — and fight to win quickly, using any effective tactic.

A favorite ploy was to turn the matter around, and blame Rebecca for provoking his bad conduct. Failing that, he'd resort to abusive name-calling. This soon escalated to breaking vases, and physical intimidation. Once, Scott slapped her. He was instantly contrite, truly aghast at how he had become like his parents. He kept his promise never to hit her again.

After that, they seldom quarreled, but Scott was remote, spending more and more time working. They separated six months later, after Rebecca discovered an affair.

Meanwhile, Jerry's good grades earned him a scholarship to college, where he met Linda in chemistry lab. She, too, is quiet and serious, but they found plenty to talk about. They discussed books and ideas. They compared unhappy family histories. They discovered a shared dream: both wanted to teach high school. Most of all, their utter lack of conflict came as a great relief to Jerry. They never raised their voices with each other.

Linda and Jerry married as soon as they graduated. Each of them won a good job offer, but in different towns. Linda was ready to defer to Jerry's opportunity, but he declined the traditional male prerogative, suggesting they draw lots. Linda picked the longer straw.

During their first year of marriage, Linda was often preoccupied with lesson plans, while Jerry had an abundance of time on his hands. Soon, Linda's enthusiasm about her work began to grate on Jerry. A couple of times, he tried to tell her how useless he felt. Her initial, sympathetic response soon turned defensive. "What do you want me to do? Quit my job? I'm under a lot of pressure, too, you know." Jerry recoiled in hurt. "Maybe it's unfair of me to spoil her excitement by complaining," he decided privately.

Jerry often caught himself feeling irritated with Linda about small matters, like the way she would sometimes finish his sentences when he paused a moment to find the right word. He tried to shrug it off, but one Friday evening, she did it twice in ten minutes. "I may not have a great job like you, but I'm still capable of a complete thought," he said icily, and stormed out the door.

When Jerry returned after a couple hours driving around, Linda was already in bed. He slept on the couch for the first time.

Both of them arise early the next morning, unable to sleep. Linda scrambles eggs for breakfast. They eat in silence. Finally, she musters the courage to speak. "We have to talk."

"About what?"

"About us. It's obvious how miserable you are. I want to help, but I can't break through your shell."

"Unless you have news about a job opening at school, I can't see where there's much to talk about."

"You don't even give me a chance to show I care. Please, talk to me."

"The last time I tried, you didn't want to hear it."

"I know. I started feeling guilty that I have a great job, when you don't. So I got defensive. I'm sorry I wasn't a good listener then, but I can do better."

"What's the use? You still might not like hearing what I'd say. I just can't stand it when you get upset at me."

"You'd rather we live like strangers? I hate arguing, too, but this is worse. I can't promise never to get upset. But even if I do, that's not the end of the world. We can get past it."

The dual example of Scott and Jerry shows the sensitizing effects of growing up in a family where conflict raged out of control. It shows how different measures of stimulation-seeking interact with family experience. From observing the model of their parents, neither Scott nor Jerry has any idea how to constructively manage conflict.

Scott, who relishes potent stimulation, will engage a conflict if pushed, despite his misgivings. He just tries to end it quickly, with a show of superior force. He fights to win, until he sees that he is becoming like his parents. Then, in horror, he withdraws.

Jerry is temperamentally averse to intense stimulation of any kind. This, in combination with his childhood conditioning, makes conflict unbearable for him. Maybe, with Linda's encouragement, he'll overcome this sensitivity enough to disprove the expectation that conflict always turns ugly.

Conflict-avoidant family of origin

From considering only the examples of Scott and Jerry, it might seem like a totally peaceable household would better enable children to contend with marital conflict in their later, adult lives. Not necessarily.

Conflict-*avoidant* parents, by their example, instill apprehensions similar to their own. If parents always sweep any dissension under the rug, their children infer that open conflict spawns calamity. They learn to fear and avoid it, just like their parents. In order to become properly equipped for later marriage, children need the model of parents who accept and resolve conflict, as it arises.[1]

However acquired, the dread of family conflict resists change, because people naturally avoid situations that could potentially disconfirm their fear. That's why tolerance for conflict is such an important qualification to bring to marriage. Conflicts are a natural part of married life. By engaging these conflicts in a spirit of good faith and commitment, we meet with some of the richest spiritual opportunities. This work is sweetened by a full measure of the crowning qualification, Appreciation for Mystery and Paradox.

Nine

Appreciation for Mystery and Paradox
*Are you willing to cherish what
you cannot fully understand or control?*

*Marriage is not only the expression of love between two people, it is
also a profound evocation of one of life's greatest mysteries, the weaving together of many different strands of soul.* —Thomas Moore[1]

To be surprised, to wonder, is to begin to understand.
—José Ortega y Gassett

Having eyes do you not see, and having ears do you not hear?
—Mark 8:18

During courtship, we are all detectives of the soul, in fevered pursuit of an elusive secret. We delve deep to uncover the source of our fascination. We carefully examine every detail. But beyond this, our quest has little in common with crime mysteries, where cool logic reigns, and satisfaction hinges on *solving* the case.

The mysteries of love permit no solution. They are akin to religious mysteries, such as the nature of God and the meaning of life. Persistent, subjective inquiry deepens our understanding, but ultimately, they are unfathomable, by nature. Therein lies the allure — at least for those with eyes to see beneath the surface and ears to hear subtle nuance. We can endlessly contemplate these mysteries, finding continual intrigue. Paradox only intensifies the appeal.

Falling in love, we plunge headlong into the realm of mystery and paradox. Then, in marriage, the plot thickens. We encounter the inexhaustible wonder of human nature, strangeness amidst familiarity, the volatile interplay of male and female, shifting needs for closeness and distance, and the grand paradox of sexuality. In order to harvest the spiritual fruit of these mysteries, we must bring to marriage an attitude of wonder and appreciation for matters that defy rational comprehension.

Romantic Enchantment

Falling in love poses one of the most beguiling — and vexing — mysteries of life. It pixilates both young and old, simple and wise. Neither worldly experience nor psychological insight affords immunity. It promises the moon, but like the moon, love's rapture waxes and wanes. Experts caution that the euphoria of falling in love amounts to a mere feeling — a fleeting rainbow that makes a shifty platform for commitment, or any major decision.

Hardly anyone heeds this warning. Why do we so readily take leave of our senses to become fools for love? Mere lust cannot account for it. Not even projective identification can explain it away. Intuitive, spiritual wisdom is at work beneath the apparent folly.

Love dangles an irresistible lure: *Infatuated lovers accept each other totally.* They detect endearing charm even in obvious faults. Such unconditional affirmation gives license for bold conduct.

When someone finds delight in even our foolishness, we can more easily risk improvisation. Released from our inhibitions, we blossom in fulfillment of love's expectation. What may have been petty or mean or ugly *actually becomes* magnanimous, kind and beautiful, in love's dominion. Which vision better represents the true identity of our beloved? Perhaps we see deeply and truly only through the bewitched eyes of love.

Alan Watts recognized how the interplay between illusion and reality works to the spiritual advantage of both parties:

> When you are in love with someone, you do indeed see them as a divine being. Now, suppose that is what they truly are and that your eyes have by your beloved been opened. . . . Through a tremendous outpouring of psychic energy in the total devotion and worship for this other person, who is respectively god or goddess, you realize by total fusion and contact, the divine center in them. At once it bounces back to you and you discover your own.[2]

Despite the spiritual potential of erotic passion, religious conservatives often regard it with suspicion. Exclusive romantic attachment seems to contradict the Christian ideal of *impartial* love. Furthermore, erotic love validates compelling personal experience over rational self-control and obedience to religious dogma. It upsets the established order, threatening to hoist "libido over credo."[3] It separates what was united, and unites what society had reason to keep separate.

Deranged lovers sacrifice critical judgment at the altar of Eros. In their preoccupation with each other, they forget everything else. They shirk inconvenient duties, and abandon prior commitments that conflict with their lovesick craving. Fortunes, reputations, even kingdoms have been lost in this passionate pursuit of union. Such moonstruck loss of control looks comical from the outside. Cynics mock it to conceal their envy.

How can we open our hearts to romantic love, without being reckless? How can we reconcile the dawning awareness of our mate's imperfections with the prior realization of her divine essence? We need not abandon all caution and good sense to engage the mysteries of love. But neither can we avoid risk entirely, except at the forfeit of our heart's desire. We must stumble forward, in joy and trepidation, without trying to force a hasty resolution of the paradox.

We may as well enjoy romance as long as possible. Only a fool would purposely break the spell. Yet, only a fool would cling to the illusion. Anticipating our certain fate, we prepare to meet it with good cheer instead of resentment. In the following example, Joe puts an ironic twist on his first big argument with Connie.

"You're so stubborn. You just won't admit when you're wrong," Connie accuses her husband.

"That's not true."

"Oh, yeah? Name one time you've admitted you're wrong."

"Hmmm." Joe is momentarily stumped. Then a triumphant smile crosses his face. "I used to think you were perfect, but now I realize I was mistaken."

Both are able to laugh at this remark, which drains the tension from their conflict. Connie picks up on the wry spirit with a comeback of her own.

"That's a start," she allows. "You may have meant it as a little slam, but it actually helps me feel better about myself."

"What do you mean?" Joe asks warily.

"I used to worry that you were smarter than me, but now it's clear I have no cause for concern. You see, I've *always* recognized *your* faults, despite being so in love with you."

No one should underestimate the hazards of romantic enchantment. Still, the unruly erotic impulse makes an essential contribution to the spiritual power of love. We cannot factor it out, in an attempt to sanitize marriage, except at the expense of emotional and spiritual vitality.

The Inexhaustible Wonder of Human Nature

Love renders everyone more interesting and attractive. At the beginning of a new relationship, sweethearts instinctively pay attention to each other, mesmerized by an exotic creature who promises so much. They discern a seductive dance in every spontaneous gesture. They hear poetry in every murmured phrase. They drink deeply — to intoxication — and yet remain unquenched.

After a few years, though, many couples complain of losing the "magic" that once inhabited their relationship. In response, parents, pastors, and drinking buddies alike advise them to lower expectations: "Welcome to the real world. Nothing lasts forever." For a fee, many professional counselors dispense equally insipid guidance.

Can marriage really inspire no greater excitement than folding laundry, mowing the lawn, and shuttling the children between soccer games and piano lessons? Many couples succumb to the stifling crush of routine. But that outcome is not intrinsic to married life. It represents a drab compromise between the sublime possibilities and the maddening aggravations that come with them.

> After only four years of marriage to Shirley, Wayne can barely recall the time, during their courtship, when he regarded her with fascination. During an individual therapy session, he complains, "She only wants to gossip. She can ramble on for an hour at a time about her friend Lisa's problems. I don't even like Lisa very much, and I just don't care about whether Lisa's boss is treating her fairly, or the trouble Lisa's kids are having at school.
>
> "I especially don't want to hear about what's going on between Lisa and her husband, Dwight. He's a buddy of mine — a really good guy. I can just tune out when Shirley drones on about Lisa, but when she drags Dwight into it, I usually end up defending him. Before long, we're fighting — about *somebody else's marriage.* It's ridiculous."

"Have you told Shirley you'd rather not hear about Lisa's problems?"

"I held back for a long time. It seemed rude. I figured she'd get the idea, if I didn't comment. But no. She interprets silence as a request for more details. Eventually, she asks outright what I think Lisa should do. Of course, when I tell her, she disagrees, and wants to argue."

"So what happened when you finally owned up to your lack of interest in Lisa's problems?"

"By then, I'd lost patience. So I probably didn't handle it very well. I said, 'Can't you see I don't give a damn about Lisa?' So then she accused me of not caring about anyone but myself."

"But you care about Shirley — or at least you used to," I remind him. "Have you ever wondered *why* she talks so much about Lisa?"

"Not really. I guess that's just the way she is. Maybe women are just different from men."

"No doubt, they are. Perhaps it's even fair to say that women usually show more interest in discussing relationships. But that generalization isn't helping you find areas of *mutual* interest. Have you ever tried to steer the conversation away from Lisa, toward topics closer to home?"

"Well, no. By the time I realize what's happening, I usually don't want to talk about *anything*. I'm just biding my time, hoping she'll get tired of basically talking to herself."

Wayne's own passivity is the major cause of his boredom. He withholds from engaging his wife constructively. Nothing prevents him from opening topics of his own choosing, or taking an assertive stand against what he *doesn't* want to hear. It's as if he expects Shirley to entertain him, or else leave him alone.

More importantly, Wayne can't muster any curiosity about his wife's perspective. Perhaps she's bored with her own life, seeking a vicarious thrill from Lisa's drama, as if from watching a soap opera. Perhaps, by listening closely, he could detect a more personal, underlying theme. Shirley would probably prefer to discuss their own relationship if he were receptive. Unfair as it may be for her to bait him with attacks on his friend Dwight, that tactic at least succeeds in getting a rise out of him.

We spark the magic in marriage not by dutiful effort, polite restraint, or lofty spiritual ambition, but through small acts of imagination and courage. On the lighter side, these include affectionate teasing and earthy humor. Equally important — although typically less welcome — we quicken our relationships by presenting inconvenient needs, expressing frank preferences and emotions, naming unpleasant truths, and challenging each other to attain our highest potentials.

When partners engage in such vital exchange, they sometimes inflame sensitivities and incite quarrels. Marriage is a contact sport. We risk occasional upset when we reach for the best it has to offer. Or else we settle for what's safe, but soon stale.

In truth, we can never capture the fullness of our mates. No one can ever possess thoroughgoing knowledge of another human being, as if he were some biological specimen, exhaustively catalogued and mounted in a display case. The complaint of boredom is invariably an excuse, covering fear or laziness. It evades intense relationship.

Deeper complexities always await discovery, if we cultivate a curious attitude toward our mates. At every turn, fresh perspectives come into view. Unfamiliar circumstances arise, evoking previously untapped potentials. Interests shift and realign. New capabilities emerge.

These processes contain the potential to stimulate ongoing interest and appeal, enabling a couple to grow in mutual comprehension over a married lifetime. Love matures as realization of each other's true identity replaces self-serving preconceptions. Human nature, as represented by a singular man or woman, forms the prototypical mystery, replete with meaning when observed through the lens of love.

Strangeness Amidst Familiarity

After living together for ten or twenty years, most couples develop an uncanny reciprocal knowledge. Each possesses a vast store of intimate information about the other, sometimes enabling them to know each other's thoughts in advance, or predict each other's reaction to some new circumstance. Over the course of a long marriage, tastes and attitudes converge. Many couples assume even a remarkable physical likeness by the time they reach their golden anniversary. This attests to deep interpenetration of souls, beyond shared diet and lifestyle.

Either party could compose the other's biography. Each has heard countless stories of formative incidents from the other's life. In addition, each partner has logged untold hours of direct observation, accumulating innumerable tidbits of personal data. Mothers know their children less thoroughly.

Some of this information finds practical application:

Eva immediately recognizes the subtle tension that creeps in around her husband's eyes when he's not telling the full truth.

Ted knows his wife's preferred bath temperature, having filled the tub for her so many times.

Other intimate knowledge holds purely sentimental value:

Bruce fondly harbors an image of exactly how his wife purses her lips when applying lipstick. This vivid mental picture springs to mind, unbidden, when she's away from home overnight on business.

Chloe treasures her husband's scent left behind on his pillow. When she makes the bed, she sometimes takes a moment to press his pillow to her face, inhaling deeply.

Seasoned couples take this profound familiarity for granted. It fosters security and comfort. But what happens when one partner manages to surprise the other? Some people strive to confine their mates to predictable responses, while others welcome fresh insights. The difference depends on the extent of appreciation for mystery and paradox.

Since Mel's retirement last year, he often accompanies his wife shopping. One day, as they carry their packages to the car, Doris notices a glazed expression on her husband's face.

"You look far away. What are you thinking about?"

Mel smiles sheepishly. "You caught me daydreaming. Did you notice the salesgirl who helped us in the last store? She reminds me of a girl named Eileen that I once had a crush on when I was about fifteen. Eileen couldn't look like that anymore, of course. After fifty years, who knows if she's still alive? I haven't thought of her in . . . I don't know how long. Seeing this young woman triggered some old memories."

"You've never mentioned Eileen. I guess you're still stuck on her, huh?" Doris teases. She is long past feeling threatened by an old flame. To the contrary, she's intrigued to observe a sparkle in Mel's eye. "Tell me more," she invites.

Sometimes, though, partners become so smug in their knowledge of each other that one will actually dispute the other's declaration of an unexpected choice.

Fred and Louise receive their sundaes from the young man behind the counter at the ice cream shop, who directs them to the self-service bar for any toppings they might wish to add.

Louise furrows her brow in disapproving amazement as she watches her husband sprinkle a generous portion of chopped nuts over his chocolate marshmallow ice cream. "What are you doing?" she demands. "In forty years, I've never seen you eat chopped nuts on ice cream. You don't like nuts."

"Sometimes I do."

"No you don't."

"Watch me," Fred suggests, with amused defiance. "I'm eating chopped pecans on my ice cream. . . . Mmmm. Tasty."

We occasionally encounter an inconsistency so glaring and in-comprehensible that we feel like we're living with a stranger.

When a hockey franchise moves to town, Helen suggests to her husband that they attend a game. She knows that Will played hockey during his youth, in Canada, but that was long before they met. During their thirty years of married life together, he has shown little interest in this or any other rugged sport. She knows him as a gentle, meekly intellectual man who spends most of his free time reading or studying the stock market.

During the hockey match, Helen discovers a side of Will that shocks and almost frightens her. He yells crude remarks at the opposing players and cheers when a fight breaks out. Who *is* this man with blood lust gleaming in his eyes? Helen feels embarrassed to sit next to him. For weeks afterwards, she feels curiously alienated, even though Will promptly reverts to his customary, mild-mannered self in their rou-tine interactions.

Helen decides to observe her husband more carefully, consciously trying to suspend the expectations that have constrained her range of perception. She begins to notice other signs of this more earthy, aggressive aspect of Will's character. Gradually, she incorporates these previously over-looked features, developing a more complete image of him, and a heightened respect for his complexity. She also *likes* him better — especially in bed.

Unsettling as it may be to uncover such startling quirks of character, they should remind us never to underestimate the boundless complexity of our mates. We realize that we may never bridge some of the gaps in our comprehension of each other. From an attitude of appreciation for mystery, this feels more refreshing than disturbing. If our mates defy our efforts to confine them to narrow boxes, how much less can we presume to have figured out the ways of God?

The Interplay of Male and Female

Both men and women routinely spout generalizations critical of the opposite sex. Men accuse women of being emotionally unstable, indecisive, irrational and vain. According to the stereotype, women also talk too much and spend too much. As Henry Higgins grumbled in *My Fair Lady*, "Why can't a woman be more like a man?"

Even Sigmund Freud threw up his hands in dismay, asking "What do women want?" This is not really a question, of course, but an attempt to *dismiss* the question by insinuating the futility of trying to please a woman. Having concluded that women are inscrutable by nature, men can excuse themselves from any further effort.

Women, for their part, complain that men are insensitive, aloof and preoccupied with proving themselves through material achievements and sexual conquests. According to the stereotype, men spend too much time watching sports on TV, at the expense of self-awareness. "They're afraid of their own feelings, and intimidated by ours. So they try to turn everything into a problem they can solve."

Despite all this carping, men and women still find each other irresistible. One adage (originally coined by men referring to women) now finds expression on both sides of the gender battlefield: "You can't live with 'em, and you can't live without 'em." Apparently, the sexes embody just enough similarity to resonate as kindred, and just enough disparity to stimulate excitement.

Biology dictates some of the distinctions: Divergent hormones equip men and women to fulfill their divergent reproductive roles, with far-reaching secondary effects. Other differences stem from cultural prescriptions, which vary widely from place to place. Even within a particular culture, gender expectations shift from time to time, especially in our modern era, driven by mass media.

In twentieth-century America, the tide turned several times, favoring androgyny in the Roaring Twenties and the Swinging Sixties, while promoting greater sex role discrepancy in between. The current tendency to highlight the dissimilarity of men and women may represent a backlash against feminist strivings for political equality, as well as mounting scientific evidence of biological distinctions.

Gender differences sometimes loom large. But in declaring the other gender fundamentally alien, we evade encounter with mystery. We do better to drop all generalizations, and strive to comprehend our mate's uniquely personal qualities. This promotes a sense of wonder that a creature so exasperatingly different from ourselves could hold such provocative appeal.

Longing for Union versus the Need for Distance

Our society pays lip service to the ideal of intimate togetherness in marriage. Yet, when the pendulum swings too far (or too fast) in that direction, we get edgy. It's unfair to categorically dismiss these restive feelings as "fear of intimacy." The soul naturally seeks a measure of distance in order to preserve its integrity in the teeth of mounting interdependence. At these times, we feel drawn toward some separate activities. Ordinarily, these corrective impulses pose no threat to marriage. The desire for union arises again, once we reaffirm our autonomy.

Problems more likely stem from trying to suppress our legitimate, periodic need for distance. When we disregard it, we may find ourselves harboring trivial secrets or picking a fight, just to assert our independence.

Lyle has been acting moody for several days. Tonight, he seems especially remote. All throughout dinner, his wife, June, tries in vain to engage him in conversation. Finally, she asks outright, "Is anything troubling you? You seem distant."

"Hmmm? Oh, I'm OK."

They finish their meal in silence. Then, just as they are getting up from the table, June remarks, "Oh, I almost forgot to mention that Peggy called this afternoon. She and Chet want us to come over for cards on Saturday. I told her we'd be there around 7:30."

"You might have checked with me before accepting," Lyle says crossly.

It's the first time all day that June has heard him string together so many words. She stops short, casserole dish in hand, halfway between the table and the refrigerator. "What has gotten into you?" she demands, wheeling to face her husband. "We've been playing bridge with this same couple for ten years. Now, suddenly, you don't want to play? Or do you have 'a prior engagement'? I'm sorry I neglected to consult your social calendar."

"You don't have to get sarcastic. I'll go along," Lyle says grudgingly.

"Well, you won't be doing the rest of us any favor, unless your mood improves. What's up with you, lately, anyway?"

"Nothing. I'm just tired of having my life all planned out for me. Maybe I don't know yet what I'll want to do on Saturday."

"Whatever. Call Peggy and Chet to let them know when you decide."

Lyle sighs audibly. He regrets his unreasonable behavior. He really doesn't know why he reacted so strongly to such a trivial matter. He only knows for sure that he feels unaccountably hemmed in.

Lyle's confusion stems from ignoring the call to interrupt the stifling insularity of his routine life. Something in him yearns to break free. "From what?" he wonders. For days, he has noticed himself reacting irritably to just about everything June says or does. He realizes she has done nothing to give offense. If anything, she has tried especially hard to please him — which annoys him all the more.

Lyle decided he couldn't, in fairness, fault June for something that apparently originates within himself. Failing to identify any good reason for feeling so peevish, he withdrew into his shell, hoping the mood would pass. Instead, it erupted in response to minor provocation.

Marriage invites us to learn how we can remain secure in ourselves at progressively deeper levels of intimacy. But we may as well admit our provisional limits at any time. When we chronically frustrate the soul's periodic need for distance, we become irritable — and more at risk of some desperate action like an affair.

Trouble brews when couples assume inflexible, polarized roles for negotiating closeness and distance. In a common pattern, one partner (typically, the woman) habitually presses for more time together, more cooperative interaction, more accountability, and especially, more self-disclosure. The other partner (typically, the man) habitually seeks more time apart, more independence, more privacy, and more emotional reserve.[4] One persistently promotes union; the other doggedly preserves necessary boundaries. One pursues; the other flees.

This pattern masks the reality that everybody needs closeness sometimes, and distance at other times. As long as we adhere to our accustomed, complementary roles, we never notice the opposing need in ourselves; we rely on our partner to serve that function. The pursuer never realizes her periodic need for distance, because her partner reliably backs away before she exceeds her tolerance for closeness. She constantly feels unwanted. Her husband never realizes his periodic need for closeness, because his partner reliably draws near before his need reaches threshold. He constantly feels smothered.

How can you escape these confining roles? Notice the dynamic tension between your desire for closeness and the opposing need for distance. Keep special watch for whichever side is less familiar. Once in a while, do something contrary to your usual stance. If you ordinarily pursue, encourage your partner to take some time away from you. If you ordinarily flee, arrange to spend some romantic time together. Besides earning gratitude from your startled mate, you'll instill vitality in your relationship, sacrificing only the dubious distinction of consistency.

Sexuality: The Grand Paradox

Sex is rife with paradox. When we contrive to impose one side of the contradiction at the expense of the other, we meet with a humbling correction. Sex will not abide our attempts at containment.

The paradox of spontaneity versus effort, mentioned earlier in regard to marriage generally, pertains even more forcefully to sex. On one hand, anyone who has been married for a few years knows the value of advance preparation. Most people find it worthwhile to devote at least a few moments to clearing their mental slate, creating a suitably receptive attitude. If a couple has young children, securing the bedroom door can make the difference between privacy and untimely interruption. Fresh sheets or a lit candle may likewise enhance the mood.

On the other hand, some of the most glorious sexual epiphanies catch us by surprise. We're apt to become attached to a preconceived outcome when we try to orchestrate sex. At the extreme, any head-strong effort to compel arousal or orgasm will more likely hinder it.

Technical proficiency confers no immunity to sexual failure, and may even evoke it. Owing to pride, sex enthusiasts are sometimes least able to cope with the performance lapses and fluctuations of desire that eventually afflict their favorite pastime. Preoccupation with performance leeches sex of its soul. Sexual complications challenge our heroic attitude, and lend ironic grace: They invite us to deeper waters, beyond the shoals of sense gratification.

Romantics often harbor sentimental notions of sex. They cherish gentle expressions of sexuality, and reject the earthy, aggressive, even nasty elements. In an old comedy routine, one fellow asks another, "What's the matter with you? Do you think sex is always dirty?" "No," comes the reply. "Only *good* sex." While this may overstate the matter, it reminds us of the folly in any campaign to sanitize sex. Sex bids us to integrate our "higher" spiritual yearnings with our equally legitimate bodily nature. Fulfillment depends on finding ways to accommodate robust abandon along with the sweetness of tender, affectionate sex.

Tolerance for Ambiguity

In order to cultivate appreciation for mystery and paradox, we must learn to relax when confronted with unfamiliar, ambiguous or even contradictory circumstances. This ability requires trust in our own ingenuity to cope with the unknown. It correlates with emotional security. People with a high tolerance for ambiguity are able to brook diversity and complexity in others, having made peace with their own inconsistencies.

Dogmatism lies at the opposite end of the continuum. People who are dogmatic insist on definitive, black-or-white answers to even the most complicated questions. Unable to come to terms with doubts and contradictions, they are quick to judge, in terms of Good or

Evil, True or False, Right or Wrong. For fear of being overwhelmed by the unknown, they are rigid, authoritarian and closed-minded. They miss the humor lurking in most situations. They disregard the subtleties of married life.

Anyone who lacks an appreciation for mystery overlooks much of the beauty and wonder of marriage, and evades much of its power. What remains soon appears dry and stale, like a withered husk. By embracing mystery, we welcome grace and serendipity into marriage. God is always at home in such company.

Thus, an appreciation for mystery and paradox rounds out the list of qualifications for marriage as a spiritual vocation. This receptive attitude arises out of willingness to simply accept what *is*, in all its irreducible complexity. We suspend our customary insistence on knowing how it works, what it is good for, and how to possess it. We find a way to sustain curiosity and amazement about matters that defy analysis or control. We surrender to transfiguring engulfment by an incomprehensible force. These are the same attitudes required for any spiritual quest.

Epilogue

Who Wants to Dance?

True love always requires great daring. —John Welwood[1]

A ll brides and grooms have high hopes on their wedding day. "Here, at last, I have found someone who will love me as no one else has ever loved me. This is someone who will understand me, cherish me and respect me; someone who will take care of me when I'm sick, and support me in pursuit of my goals — which now become *our* goals. I can count on my new partner to support me emotionally, as well, lifting my spirits when I'm down, standing by me when others turn away. No less important, this is someone receptive to all I offer in return. Together, we'll find personal and spiritual fulfillment, as we draw out the best in each other. Our mutual fascination will last a lifetime, and our love will never end."

Ultimately, these romantic longings are not so foolish as they might appear. But the path to bliss leads through disappointment and conflict. Many couples get lost there, lose heart, and abandon the quest. Others recognize the end of the honeymoon as the beginning of their spiritual work together. Having read this far, you are probably among them.

As you have seen, the spiritual potential of marriage does not depend on religious piety. Nor is your fate sealed by the choice of the right or wrong partner. You can start wherever you are. All you need is willingness. So consider, once again, the questions posed at the beginning of this section:

1. Are you willing to live consciously, claiming full responsibility for your life?
2. Are you willing to admit your limitations, your need for change and for help?
3. Are you willing to ardently pursue deeper knowledge of your mate, and likewise open your heart for inspection?
4. Are you willing to bear the strain of conflict?
5. Are you willing to cherish what you cannot fully understand or control?

If so, you're ready for the spiritual vocation of marriage. Strengthened by these essential commitments, you can approach the natural ups and downs of relationship more creatively. You'll see that differences become occasions for intimacy. Problems become openings to grace.

So take up the Sacred Dance, and pour your heart into it. You and your mate will come to know yourselves and each other more intimately than you could have imagined. Along the way, you will transcend yourselves and join company with God.

Bibliography

Buber, Martin, *I and Thou*. New York: Macmillan, 1958.

Campbell, Joseph, *The Power of Myth*. New York: Doubleday, 1988.

Chang, Jolan, *The Tao of Love and Sex*. New York: E. P. Dutton, 1977.

Fisher, Helen E., *Anatomy of Love*. New York: W.W. Norton, 1992.

Fromm, Erich, *The Art of Loving*. New York: Harper & Row, 1956.

Hendrix, Harville, *Getting the Love You Want: A Guide for Couples*. New York: Henry Holt, 1988.

Holy Bible (Revised Standard Version), New York: Thomas Nelson and Sons, 1952 (Old Testament) and 1946 (New Testament).

Hunter, David G., *Marriage in the Early Church*. Minneapolis: Fortress Press, 1992.

Johnson, Robert A., *We: Understanding the Psychology of Romantic Love*. San Francisco: Harper & Row, 1983.

Keating, Thomas, *Intimacy with God*. New York: The Crossroad, 1996.

Margulis, Lynn & Sagan, Dorion, *Mystery Dance: On the Evolution of Human Sexuality*. New York: Summit Books, 1991.

Maurer, Harry, *Sex: An Oral History*. New York: Viking Penguin, 1994.

McBrien, Richard P., *Catholicism*. Minneapolis: Winston Press, 1981.

Miller, Alice, *The Drama of the Gifted Child*. New York: Basic Books, 1983.

Moore, Thomas, *Care of the Soul*. New York: HarperCollins, 1993.

———, *Soul Mates: Honoring the Mysteries of Love and Relationship*. New York: HarperCollins, 1994.

Oliver, Mary Anne McPherson, *Conjugal Spirituality: the Primacy of Mutual Love in Christian Tradition*. Kansas City: Sheed & Ward, 1994.

Paglia, Camille, *Sexual Personae*. New York: Vintage Books, 1991. (Originally, by Yale University Press, 1990.)

Priests for Equality, *The Inclusive New Testament*. Brentwood, MD: Priests for Equality, 1994.

Ranke-Heinemann, Uta, *Eunuchs for the Kingdom of Heaven*. (English translation by Peter Heinegg.) New York: Doubleday, 1990.

Robinson, Jonathan (editor), *The Experience of God*. Carlsbad, CA: Hay House, 1998.

Sanford, John A., *The Invisible Partners*. Mahwah, NJ: Paulist Press, 1980.

Schillebeeckx, Edward, *Marriage: Human Reality and Saving Mystery*. (English translation by N. D. Smith.) London: Sheed & Ward, 1965.

Schnarch, David M., *Constructing the Sexual Crucible*. New York: W. W. Norton, 1991.

———, *Passionate Marriage*. New York: W. W. Norton, 1997.

Tannahill, Reay, *Sex in History* (Revised Edition). London: Scarborough House, 1992.

Timmerman, Joan, *Sexuality and Spiritual Growth*. New York: The Crossroad, 1992.

Vatsyayana (Alain Danielou, translator), *The Complete Kamasutra*. Rochester, VT: Park Street Press, 1994.

Welwood, John (ed.), *Challenge of the Heart*. Boston: Shambala, 1985.

———, *Journey of the Heart*. New York: HarperCollins, 1990.

———, *Love and Awakening*. New York: HarperCollins, 1996.

Notes

Part One

1 *Familiaris Consortio* (Apostolic Exhortation on the Family), *L'Osservatore Romano*, English Edition: vol. 14, Dec. 21–28, 1981, p. 11.

Chapter 1

1 Russian Orthodox priest, writing in *Fragments of a Diary 1881–1934*, cited in Oliver, p. 53.
2 George Lichtenberg, an eighteenth-century German satirist, coined this aphorism.

Chapter 2

1 This and all other Bible quotations are taken from the Revised Standard Version, unless another translation is specified.
2 Abridged from Matthew 22:37–39 (originally appearing in Deuteronomy 6:5 and Leviticus 19:18, respectively). Jesus cited these two "Great Commandments" as the foundation and summary of all the Jewish Law and Prophets.
3 Consider, for example, Jacob, King David, Francis of Assisi, John of the Cross, and Teresa of Avila.

4 According to biblical accounts, this was the case with Moses, for example, and with Mary, the mother of Jesus.
5 Matthew 16:25.
6 Luke 10:25–37.
7 P. 40.
8 These early experiences also provide the child's first impression of God.
9 Psychologists use the term *introjection* to characterize how we adopt the same attitude toward ourselves as our caretakers demonstrated toward us during childhood.

Chapter 3

1 Schnarch, *Passionate Marriage*, p. 403.

Chapter 4

1 The Latin root, *vocare*, means "to call."
2 Oliver, *Conjugal Spirituality*, p. 60.
3 Oliver, *Conjugal Spirituality*, p. 1.
4 Oliver, *Conjugal Spirituality*, p. 24.
5 Ephesians 5:28 (Inclusive New Testament).
6 "And in that day, says the Lord [when Israel renounces idolatry and renews faithfulness to God]...you will call me 'My Husband'". (Hosea 2:16)
7 Hunter, *Marriage in the Early Church*, pp. 13–18.
8 In the average major city during that era, one prostitute plied her trade for every dozen men between the ages of 15 and 60 (Tannahill, *Sex in History*, p. 356).
9 Welwood, *Love and Awakening*, p. 243.

Part Two

1 The Inclusive New Testament.
2 Schnarch, *Passionate Marriage*, p. 49.

Chapter 5

1 Moore, *Soul Mates*, p. 24.
2 Thomas Moore elaborates a wealth of similar practices in *Care of the Soul*.
3 Of course, the individual response to misfortune determines each particular outcome. Some hardy souls manage to rise above circumstances that would crush the average person. Either way, though, it's foolish to discount the impact of childhood adversity.
4 At the opposite extreme, some parents offer misguided support by insisting, "You can become anything you want." A moment's reflection exposes the fallacy of this claim. Insurmountable obstacles are everywhere. Not every child who dreams of becoming an astronaut possesses the right stuff. Even gifted athletes encounter a very limited professional job market. When these harsh facts of life impose limitations, children who were given grandiose expectations can only attribute the failing to personal inadequacy. They become ashamed to dream. More fairly, we could encourage youngsters to "Pursue your dreams with all your strength. It will be worth the effort, whatever the outcome."

Chapter 6

1 In pointing out the futility of this shame-driven striving, I do not mean to deny the virtue of continually aspiring to excellence

in deed and in character. Lofty goals are fine, as long as we remember the two Principles of Perfection: It is unattainable; and our worthiness of love does not depend on it.

2 In more severe cases, physical abuse also represents a discharge of distorted shame.

3 A mere thirty years ago, my graduate training in clinical psychology at a leading university included not a single reference to shame.

Chapter 7

1 Campbell, *The Power of Myth*, pp. 200–201.

2 Fisher, *Anatomy of Love*. The author marshals anthropological evidence to show how evolutionary forces drive an intriguing range of phenomena, including jealousy, variation in penis size and testicle size among different primate species, the relative body mass of males and females, and the voluptuous breasts and orgasms of human females.

3 In 1965, the Second Vatican Council adopted the covenant as the model for sacred matrimony within the Roman Catholic Church (McBrien, p. 791).

4 Jeremiah 7:23.

5 Miller, *The Drama of the Gifted Child*.

6 Of course, girls also suffer parental neglect and abuse, with no less devastating consequences. Their coping strategies tend to differ, though. It's relatively uncommon for females to disavow subjective life — and the yearning to share it in relationship — in favor of identifying with their achievements. Traditionally, our culture has made this route less available to females. Women are much more likely than men to persist in revealing their vulnerability, despite repeated neglect or exploitation. Instrumental thinking in the service of emotional guardedness is a characteristically masculine strategy.

7 Having formed such porous boundaries, women are prone to sacrifice too much for the sake of relationship. Rushing headlong into intimacy, they sometimes jeopardize their separate identity.

8 Of course, a man can circumvent the entire issue by holding back from falling in love. This was Ralph's approach. Recognizing the practical advantages of marriage, he simply shopped for a suitable wife, applying the same criteria he might use when seeking a business partner.

Chapter 8

1 This is not to say that parents should put every argument on display. Some issues, such as the parents' sexual relationship, are inherently personal. Couples should discuss these matters privately. The same holds true for conflicts about how to discipline the children, lest they exploit their parents' difference of opinion.

Parents should also take into account the child's age. Toddlers naturally feel threatened by any sign of disharmony. Small children may also have trouble discerning when a conflict is resolved. So they deserve some sheltering, if possible. By the time children reach school age, though, they can benefit from observing their parents settle conflicts, even if the process looks a bit ragged.

Chapter 9

1 Moore, *Soul Mates*, p. 45.
2 From *Play to Live*, reprinted in Welwood, *Challenge of the Heart*, p. 22.
3 Campbell, *The Power of Myth*, p. 187.

4 Ironically, this *domestic* arrangement reverses the traditional *courtship* roles (still widely observed) in which men are expected to take the initiative. The courtship pattern carries over into domestic life only with regard to sex. Hence the familiar complaint of women in traditional relationships: "You only approach me when you want sex."

Epilogue

1 Welwood, *Love and Awakening*, p. 20.

About the Author

Dr. Larry Wampler is a licensed psychologist and marriage counselor in private practice, emphasizing the integration of psychological and spiritual wisdom. Over the course of his thirty year career, he has helped hundreds of couples resolve marital conflicts and realize the spiritual opportunities of marriage.

He graduated Phi Beta Kappa with a BA from the University of Oregon. He earned a Ph.D. in psychology from Vanderbilt, where he studied under the renowned pioneer of psychotherapy research, Hans H. Strupp. Dr. Wampler completed his internship at the University of California, Davis, Medical Center, and worked at both the University of California, Los Angeles, and the University of Southern California.

Dr. Wampler speaks to audiences at churches and community centers and on college campuses. He has served as a consultant to St. Francis Seminary, at the University of San Diego, where he taught programs in family relations and human sexuality, and led discussion groups. He has also presented seminars to Catholic clergy and ordained deacons in the San Diego Diocese.

Dr. Wampler's respect for the wisdom of other religious traditions lends depth and broad appeal to his writing. In addition to his academic study of world religions, he practiced Buddhist Insight Meditation for many years before returning to his Christian roots. Inspired by the spirituality of his wife, Kathy, he converted to Catholicism. They have been married twenty-three years, and reside in the California coastal town of Encinitas.

For more information about the author, or to order this book online, visit www.drlarrywampler.com.